Seven Ways Benefit You.

"A Child's Palette":

- introduces a simple yet profound programme to help kids feel good about themselves and others

- discusses why children suffer and what you can do about it

- examines childhood roots of complexes and how to resolve them

- suggests what to do if a child feels unloved: some simple yet powerful awareness skills

- presents inspiring ways to relate to children

- reviews what children can teach you about you, them and life

- provides strategies to release family and classroom stress and tension

"A Child's Palette"

BUILDING BETTER RELATIONSHIPS WITH CHILDREN

By
RICKIE HILDER

Published in Sydney, Australia 2000

Rickie Hilder
P.O. Box 941
Kensington
Sydney   2033
Australia
Fax +61 (0)2 9399 9820
Email   kwanyin33@hotmail.com
Webpage www.chilli.net.au/~kwanyin/

Copyright © Rickie Hilder 2000

All rights reserved. No part of this book may be reproduced or transmitted in any form or by any means, electronic or mechanical, including photocopying, recording or by any information storage and retrieval system, without prior permission in writing from the author.

National Library of Australia
Cataloguing-in-Publication data:

Hilder, Rickie.
A Child's Palette : building better relationships with children

1st ed.
Bibliography.
ISBN 0 646 39285 9

1. Children and adults.2. Color – Psychological aspects. 3. Parent and child. 4. Self-esteem in children. I. Title.
305.231

Contents

ix Acknowledgements

x Introduction

12 Preface
Includes comments from children and adults who have participated in Rickie's sessions and workshops.

31 1 Children are the future
Reading this book could be the first step to a different life for you or your child. Every child is valuable and the life of each child matters. We discuss creating an environment where children can grow and develop in a world that appreciates and encourages difference.

44 2 Patterns
Use the Pattern to gain insights into how children and adults approach tasks and their personal strengths. Are they a leader? Are they a mediator? Does the individual see the bigger picture? Are they good at detail? Guidelines to have children subtly experience the power of the mind and the power of words. This chapter includes five Pattern case studies.

75 3 The Starchild
Introduces a Values Programme illustrating how to work with children alone or in groups, at home or school, to develop a sense that they are unique, cherished and valued. It includes step-by-step procedures to determine values which are put into practice with an Action Plan.

97 4 Your True Colours
Identifies the need to recognise ourselves and our special qualities, and opens possibilities of colours being used as keys. In a world where 'big is better', 'more is better', 'get it right' and 'keep up', children and adults lose their self-esteem. They try to be what they are not and lose their identity.   Discover your true colours and gifts.

The Colour Chapters
Every chapter on colour has practical information including gifts and challenges, together with case studies. Each colour presents keys to a deeper understanding of relationships with children, family, friends and colleagues.

106 5 Red
Red is about passion, drive and action. It holds possibilities for determination and perseverance.

116 6 Pink
Pink is about being loved as we are.

125 **7** Orange
Orange reveals enthusiasm, vitality and interest in life. It is about connection with others.

135 **8** Coral
Coral has a natural curiosity and spontaneity. It can be community minded.

141 **9** Gold
Gold is about the value we learn to put on ourselves. It reveals a positive approach to life.

151 **10** Yellow
Yellow has a sunny disposition and is interested and discerning. It is often quick-witted.

159 **11** Olive Green
Olive Green combines strength and vulnerability. It is genuinely well intentioned.

166 **12** Emerald Green
Emerald Green indicates renewal, growth and change. It is about the truth and the heart.

178 **13** Turquoise
Turquoise can be progressive and idealistic.

184 **14** Blue
Blue speaks of trust, loyalty and dedication.

194 **15** Royal Blue
Royal Blue thinks differently and can create a world in their mind.

204 **16** Violet
Violet people often have a quiet bearing and dignity. They may be shy and unassuming.

215 **17** Magenta
Magenta is charming, graceful and refined.

229 **18** Deep Magenta
Deep Magenta people can be inspirational to those around them. They are highly insightful.

234 **19** Clear
Clear has purity, innocence and simplicity. It is able to see the perspective of others.

243 **20** Conclusion
This chapter provides suggestions as to how we can make the world a better place for children, adding meaning to their lives and ensuring they are filled with hope and a sense of their worth.

Acknowledgements

I have so many reasons to be grateful, and people to thank. I would like to acknowledge and express gratitude to the adults and children who have shared their lives and experiences with me during the course of my work. I have learned as much from them as I have taught.

My heartfelt thanks go to Sandra and Gerard McCarthy of Creative Resources and Education in Sydney. I count myself as fortunate to have received their support, wisdom and guidance as counsellors, and have gained invaluable knowledge from the workshops they give.

For his support, patience and generosity in editing this material, thanks go to David Smith. For their creative input into the book, I thank the designer Lisa Salmon of Sydney and Jenette Youngman in Melbourne for the cover.

Introduction

I would, first of all, like to say in this introduction how grateful I am that Rickie has produced this work. It may sound peculiar to begin an introduction with gratitude, but this intensity I feel because I know that, as you read through the content of her work, you too will become aware of how she sees the future for us all in the hands of our children. I share this vision and it is from this understanding that my gratitude extends.

Rickie has an incredible sense of light and warmth, of humour and well-being in the way in which she presents her work in the world. The flavour she has presented with this work also draws on the many threads of her background. These threads are the resources that give to her the insights which come through the words, through the experiences. In what she shares, not only in the text but also in the case studies, we find an enriching part of our processes which help us to understand the child within ourselves more deeply.

Colour is an incredible tool to access the deeper levels within ourselves. It is with this understanding that Rickie presents something which is clear and simple and yet profound in relation to the understanding of colour. This information is clearly put, simply expounded and through which the work with colour and light may reach many hitherto untouched by some of its deeper implications.

May this book bring benefit to all those who come in contact with it.

Mike Booth

Aura-Soma International Academy of Colour Therapeutics
Lincolnshire
England
November, 1999

Preface

After I finished writing this book I gave the manuscript to various people to read and it was suggested that I tell some of my story, and say why and how I came to be doing this work with children and colour. I wondered about this and hesitated at first because I thought it is my work that is important, not my story. And yet when I am deciding whether to read a book or not, it is some connection with the author or their individual perspective that has led me to read what they have to say. Some comment, theme or suggestion sparks interest.

I believe that it is the richness of our lives' events and personal experiences that form part of what we have to give others. The combination of our qualities, values and beliefs together with that which we have learned on our life's journey through our education, encounters, thoughts, impressions and feelings, all create our individual tapestry. We learn in many ways, and in many ways we teach

So I am writing again and wondering which parts will be edited, which parts will make the final cut and what is relevant to a reader of this book. In fact my entire story is relevant, because without every step of my life, the highs and lows which contain the experiences and the mistakes which taught me so much, there would be no book. Without all these events I would not have the knowledge I have today. It was my personal need for answers and peace of mind, which led me to gather information and skills that have proved useful to others. I was able to widen my horizons, expand the work I was doing, and increase my contribution. This was particularly the work with children, and helping them to understand the importance of their self-esteem and belief that they matter as individuals.

Here is a glimpse of my journey to write this book.

I was born in Sydney, Australia during World War 2, and am the eldest of four daughters. I am told that as a very small child I was outgoing and friendly and loved to sing to people. I remember hearing an anecdote of being with my parents in a takeaway fish and chip shop, and sitting on the counter singing and entertaining the customers while we waited for our fish to be cooked. The love of music stayed with me, and I have been a professional singer and entertainer for thirty-eight years.

My mother was 19 years old when I was born, and my father 25. My first sister arrived when I was 22 months. I recall perceiving that my mother did not have time for me any more once my sister arrived, she was too busy, and that somehow I was out in the cold. Over time I learned to control my needs and did not speak or say how I really felt because I believed it would not be of any use. I have wondered many times about the impact on my mother of having two small children when she was quite young herself. I can only imagine how challenging this would have been.

Whether my mother was busy or not, the effect on me of this early childhood was to believe I was not loved as much as my sister who received the attention, which I construed as love. I loved my mother and wanted her to love me. And I tended to compare myself with the favoured child and wonder what was wrong with me. I wasn't sure what it was, but I wasn't important enough to be given as much focus. In fact this went on for years, where I saw my sister as the favourite, and that I needed to 'do something' to get noticed. So I became an achiever who tried hard at everything, seeking the approval of my parents.

My father impressed on me that I was responsible for my younger sisters. As a result I grew into someone who believed that taking full responsibility for others was part of my role in life, but underneath being angry about it. Moreover I did not know I was angry, as anger was an emotion about which I had already developed negative beliefs. I had learned that it was not okay for girls to be angry, and that I should be a 'good' girl. If I was angry I believed I was a 'bad girl', so I repressed my anger. Whatever the cause, the result of all this early conditioning was to set a pattern where I tried to take care of everything for everyone and blocked my own needs and feelings. It has been an ongoing process learning to recognise what I need and am feeling, and sometimes I am still unaware. I've needed to learn to strike a balance between caring for myself and caring for other people, and to trust others enough to allow the growth that comes with taking responsibility for the self.

My father had a lively sense of humour, a generous nature, and was free from any racial or religious prejudice. He came from a family of eleven children and had a deep loyalty to his brothers and sisters. His was a positive attitude and from him I learned that anything is possible. He was also a gambler who loved horseracing and he would go to the races, frequently losing his money. I could tell by his mood and the way he came in the front door whether I would get a belting or not. I recall being very small and hearing his key in the door, worrying about what would happen. If he lost at the races there would often be tense silences between my mother and father. If he won he would be in a happy mood and tell us stories that made us laugh. As an adult I can only imagine what it was like for my mother having four children and the financial instability which comes from living with a gambler. I know that the impact of this situation on me as a child, was an underlying anxiety and a sense of insecurity.

My childhood memories of my mother were of a good-hearted, generous and friendly woman. When I was six years old my mother became seriously ill after contracting diphtheria, so my younger sister and I were sent to live with an auntie and uncle. It was a frightening experience to be sent away from home. My uncle had returned from World War 11 with problems associated with violence. It was while living with them that I suffered sexual abuse at the hands of my uncle. The abuse was so traumatizing that I blocked it out for many years. I spoke to my father about it before he died, and he cried. This whole experience induced deep fear, difficulties with trust, and set up issues of shame, not to mention underlying outrage at the violation of guardianship.

As a child I was fearful of my father's rages, a fear heightened by the fact that I did not know when he would erupt. We had a razor-strap hanging on the kitchen wall and I was belted with this. A razor-strap is used to sharpen old fashioned cut throat razors, and it is made from very thick, strong leather. It is extremely intimidating as a child to be threatened with a 'flogging', as my father would call it, and very painful to be hit this way. It is also frightening to see another child being hit. I remember hiding behind the lounge away from my father. I wondered what I was doing that was bad enough to be punished with a razor-strap.

My father was very strict and controlling as I was growing up, and my girlfriends were allowed to do things, for example wear lipstick or stockings, before I was. I was not allowed to talk to boys and felt shame about my natural unfolding interest in the opposite sex. Love was never expressed to me by my father. In fact the first time that my father told me he loved me was on Christmas Day when I was 46 years old, and the moment stands out in my memory as one of joy. In other words my basic need to know I was loved as a child was not met, and this deficit need was something I tried to fill with other relationships during my life. Satisfying this need, however, could not happen of course, because no one can give us what we did not get as a child. It is our responsibility as adults to get our needs met, not expecting a surrogate mother or father to make it up to us.

What makes me the way I am in my family, and different from others? I know my mother and father loved me and gave me the very best they could: I do not doubt this. Even though I was part of quite a big family, I often felt lonely and that somehow I did not belong, that I was an outsider. Feeling lonely does not depend on how many people surround you. For me it was a sense of not being understood or heard, and not being able to put this into words. I know that as a child I tried to be what my parents wanted me to be in order to be loved. This became a pattern in my life, being what I thought others wanted me to be, and I often wondered why I was behaving this way, and who I really was. It was as though I could only be myself when I was alone or with a few select individuals. This set up a limited and restricted life.

All the time I knew there was more. And seeking more led me into studying, reading, questioning, and listening to the thoughts and wisdom of others. This began a life long search, which still goes on. My search took me to the United States and the United Kingdom, learning from many others, both teachers and fellow students. I am still learning and I still take classes.

I was looking for something, call it acceptance, love, to be understood, and to understand other people and myself. It was this search that led me to authors like Pia Mellody, John Bradshaw, Thomas Moore, Gary Zukav, Carl Jung, M. Scott Peck, Abraham Maslow, Viktor Frankl, and many others. Their insights about the human condition touched chords within me, and their life experiences rang true. Books became my companions and frequently the words of an author provided precisely the knowledge and encouragement I needed at a particular moment. I read voraciously and learned so much from the wisdom, awareness, and discernment of others. I have always been a curious person wanting to know 'why', and am passionate about passing this information on so that others may benefit by having answers and insights as well. Thanks go to those who have given so generously by their expression in books, and although I have given mention to various titles and authors in my Bibliography, there are many others whose titles I have lost over time.

During these years of seeking I was working and achieving goals, travelling, and entertaining on cruise ships. I won 6 Australian MO Awards, the only woman ever to win in my category, appeared on TV, and sang in nightclubs in Japan, England, Spain, Ireland, Africa and Germany. Something I noticed while travelling, is that basically we are much the same, we have similar issues and want the best for our lives. We view situations and events through our own eyes and in this we are different, and yet there are threads of commonality which link us. Many people are looking for something. I've said, and heard others ask, 'What is it all about?' 'What am I doing here?' 'My life is busy and yet it doesn't mean much. Why?' At some time in their lives a great number of people experience doubt, perhaps lack of meaning or purpose, or wonder where they fit into the scheme of things. This happens in a variety of ways, as we are all different.

The more I read, studied and observed, the more I saw how this all begins at the beginning, in childhood, where our perceptions of ourselves and our place in the world are formed, and how these beliefs influence so much of our lives. I found the roots of my beliefs and behaviour began in my childhood, and I could see that very often these old beliefs were now governing my life and how I perceived my role. I needed to find out what I was really like, and what I could do to give meaning to my life, not just at work, but as part of my daily experience. I really needed to be living my life in accordance with my values, and contributing more to the world around me. Colour was a very effective and beneficial tool to actualize these goals, and after studying in Australia I went to England to further my education and studied to be a teacher of colour to Advanced Levels.

I found the understanding of colour a remarkable, practical and fascinating resource which gave eye-opening insights. I could use it as a guide to gaining awareness of other people and their perceptions and possibilities. I discovered that the information colour offered, assisted me in gaining recognition of, and appreciation for the perspective of other individuals and their viewpoint. It fired a passion to encourage others to move beyond the limitations of their blocks, and into developing an attitude of living with their values in simple practical everyday ways: of encouraging others to give something to the world that only they can give.

In 1977 my ex-husband died suddenly, and it was a very difficult and sad time. How was I to tell our son who was six years old at the time? How was I to deal with the inexpressible loss of his father to a small child? Fortunately, as fate would have it, the day before he died I noticed an article in the newspaper reporting a newly formed association dealing with grief and loss following the Granville train disaster. I telephoned the number given in the paper and spoke to a compassionate gentleman who gave me some extremely practical, caring and sound advice. One suggestion amongst others was not to hide my grief from our son but to be open about it, in effect giving him permission to have his grief too. I read widely seeking solace and guidance, including the works written around that time by Dr. Elizabeth Kubler-Ross.

From adversity comes something that we can give to another, and my colour studies, together with my Diploma in Counselling and Communication provided extensive resources when, subsequently, I facilitated on a programme for children suffering loss of a parent through death or divorce. Very many marriages end in separation or divorce. Often the various losses that children suffer in these situations are disenfranchised: that is to say people do not recognise them as a loss, and so the child cannot express the impact and the associated feelings, whether sadness, anger, pain or fear. And there can be multiple losses, for example, the loss of grandparents, extended family, school, friends, home, social networks, security or trust. This lack of recognition and completion, sets up situations where children often act these feelings out instead, or they are buried, only to surface later in teenage or adult life causing disruption and concern. Frequently one feeling masks another, for instance underneath anger or fear, there can be hurt or sadness. The stories are different, but the pain is the same.

I have been invited to work with children and colour both privately and within classroom situations in the public and Catholic school systems in Australia and Japan. Feedback from teachers indicated surprise at the level of insights into each child after one session using colour. Initially I found the feedback from the children with whom I worked remarkable because what I was doing was very simple, and involved talking to them while they were working with the colours and creativity. Children learn on so many levels, and in numerous situations they 'learn their teacher'. This is a huge responsibility, impacting on both teachers and children. For your interest I'll include some of the remarks made by both teachers and children from Australia and Japan as they speak for themselves and tell their experience of my work. Also I will include comments from adults who have taken the workshop I give based on the contents of this book.

Their teachers asked children the following questions in the days following my visit.

Question. What do you feel you learned from participating in the session with Rickie Hilder?

Some children talked about how everyone is special, for example:

> "I felt that everyone's special in their own way and they can be creative."
>
> Rachel 8

Some commented on how they had realized something about themselves:

> "I was much more 'real-er' than I was before...I got to learn who I really am".
>
> Katie 9

> "I felt I was really gifted and special."
>
> James 8

Still other children commented on how others saw them:

> "I was glad to know how people see me as a person."
>
> Rina   12

> "In the workshop people told me what kind of person I am and I was very happy each word they said.   Also I was glad to know how people see me as a person."
>
> Aya   13

Question. What were your thoughts or feelings as you were doing it?

Some talked about themselves. For example, Tristan said he felt,

> "...happy because it's my own creative way and other people did theirs different...happy 'cause I did it my own way...nobody does everything right – we all make mistakes – we accept everybody's different like my picture's different."
>
> Tristan   11

Others spoke about the activity itself:

> "Fun, exciting – should do these activities more often because they make you think about other people and you're doing something which makes you feel happy."
>
> Rebecca 11

> "Thought it was fun and she was teaching us to imagine things and create what we think and not what other people think...to use our own ideas and talent and how good kids can be."
>
> Adam 12

Brendan summed up lots of students' comments when he said,

> "I felt like I could let all my feelings out and all my talent and I had great fun."
>
> Brendan 9

Question. "How did you feel when the class members were saying creative words about you or you were saying creative words about them?"

Most students in answering this question spoke about positive feelings. For example:

> "Well I felt happy, and how much you can all relate to each other."
>
> Dayna 9

> "I thought how nice it was to say it out loud, to say it to other people instead of keeping it to yourself."
>
> Kate 8

> "I felt special, I felt a bit funny inside cause I wasn't used to hearing those things about me."
>
> James 8

> John Pierre: "I felt….. like….unusual… but you never knew that
> Teacher: "So you never knew about yourself?"
> John Pierre: " I didn't have a clue."
>
> John Pierre 8

> "I thought for the people getting their go, I thought it was funny how people were just expressing their feelings in school in front of everyone."
>
> Gemma 8

Question.   "Did you think about the lesson any more after it, like later in the day or at any other time?"

Tristan's response to this question was very interesting. He said:

> "I thought about it a lot. I even had a dream about it last night and thought about lots of colours and some colours I've never seen before, even colours that aren't invented. Well the sun was setting across the road from my house and I was walking home then all these colours came out of the sun and flashed past my face. I went up into the sky and different colours said hello to me. When I woke up I felt happy and felt I could

> come to school and feel safe and I could trust my friends. Oh I forgot to tell you a part of the dream. 'Cause my friends faces came out of the colours – like Michael came out of the red colour, and Danielle came out of the orange and Matthew came out of the blue and they were happy and said 'hello' so I knew when I woke up I could trust them and we would be happy together. I've never had a dream like this before – it was so real."
>
> Tristan 11

Some children talked about home. For example Laura and Ian said:

> "Yes. I've been telling my mum and my dad and my family about the workshop and how it was really good."
>
> Laura 8

> "Yes, I wanted to do the same work at home."
>
> Ian 9

Chanel spoke for many other children when she enjoyed being affirmed.

> "Yep, I want to do it again because it was really fun and she told us that there was nobody the same. I think that the creativity workshop was great and I really enjoyed people saying nice things about me. Thanks I loved it."
>
> Chanel 9

Nicole has thought about her relationships with other children:
> "Since the lesson I think how to treat other people – like with the two words 'help' and 'friend'. I think if I treat others like this they'll return it back".
>
> Nicole 12

Question. What about at our school? What if Miss Hilder could do this lesson with every class?

> "Everyone would become nice to each other and learn to say nice things about each other."
>
> Rebecca 10

Themes similar to those raised in the students' comments were also reflected by the teachers. They also commented on the professional insights they gained from the workshops.

> "After working with children from 5-12 years of age at my school, Rickie's amazing insights into aspects of individual children's social, emotional and intellectual development were invaluable."
>
> Janelle
> School Principal

> "Participating with the children in the workshop I was able to see them in a completely different way. Rickie created a different space for them to be who they were. She provided me with a basis in

which to begin a different level of teaching – where the children are listened to."

Bernadette Teacher

"The workshop was very informative. Not only did I learn about myself on a personal, level, I learnt things which will help me professionally. I was provided with information on the inner level regarding personal ideas of the children in my class. Thank you." Sue Teacher

"I came because through my job as a kindergarten teacher I wanted to learn more. This seminar was very interesting. Through this seminar I could realize that I could go on in my life with confidence like I want without feeling burdened by my past. Thank you very much. I feel that I can nurture my small children with love.

Shuko Tokyo

In the workshops I have given there have been individuals who were born and raised in various countries for instance Australia, England, Japan, Greece, Ireland, America, Germany, New Zealand and Switzerland and all have related to this work. There are many issues, which are universal and easily described and recognised through colour. Here are some comments from people in different roles and occupations.

"My experience was understanding myself at a much deeper level. I now also have a much deeper understanding for others and where they are coming from."

Judith Kidby,
Customer Service Officer and Mother

"The benefits of this workshop for me were seeing why I have acted as I have in the past and gaining tools to move forward in my life and accept myself as I am. Also gaining compassion for others when you realise why they behave as they behave. A life changing experience."

Veronica Murdoch,
Pharmacist.

"The workshop helped to put me in touch with my feelings…to understand what gives meaning to my life, what I should let go, and what I should be aiming for to make me happy."

Lynette Farrugia,
Business Consultant

"When I finished Rickie's workshop, I wanted everyone to have the opportunity of sharing what she shared with us in her insightful, caring and joyful way. If every child, parent, teacher, carer, healer could have these simple yet truly profound tools, what a difference it would make. They are the keys to freedom. Rickie's workshop can change your life and the way you relate to others."

Marg Simon,
Company Director

It is December, 1999 at the time of writing this Preface, and we are at the close of a millenium. My journey has taught me that my attitudes and early beliefs were learned, and I could change these at any time to be in line with deeper perceptions. It is a matter of choice and personal responsibility. I learned that it was my attitude to my aliveness and feelings that kept them stifled, and how I had beliefs that some feelings were okay and some were not. I can shift these paradigms at any time and balance my feelings with my thoughts.

I learned that events can happen to us in our lives over which we seem to have no control, yet it is our attitude to these events, rather than the events themselves, that is important. We can perceive ourselves as victims and believe we are owed something, or accept what has happened, and move on. We can feel the full range of feelings about these events, and then choose the feelings, thoughts and attitudes with which we will stay. Ultimately it is up to us.

My wish for children in the new millenium is that they live in an environment where they are safe, where they know they are cherished, and where they have a sense that they are valuable and of worth. I hope that this sense of their worth leads them into living life in accordance with their true values, whilst appreciating the rights and values of others. I hope they recognise the importance of their contribution to society, that they have something to offer which is unique, and that this applies to everyone else as well. I hope they know in their hearts that they matter and deserve to be treated with respect, and that they treat others the same way.

I hope that their lives are filled with joy, purpose, enthusiasm, gratitude and love. I wish the same for you.

I am optimistic about the future and these next chapters of my life and work. I wish the same for you. It is not that life goes along smoothly on an even keel. Far from it. It is more a journey of discovery, adventure and growth, with all that this entails, and trusting the process of my life, step by step, as it expands rather than contracts. For me this has been a continual evolving, rather than an event My journey has certainly given me more compassion and tolerance for others.

Due to the concepts I have embraced, I have more energy, more aliveness, more joy, and more love. I wish the same for you.

I know that books containing not only information, but also the experience of others, have been of untold value to me in times of confusion and doubt I am grateful to have been able to open a book in a moment of need, and found an answer to a question. If this book answers one question for you, then my purpose is complete, because I wish the same for you.

It is important to remember, however, that the intention of this book is that it is used as a guide to exploring possibilities. I stress that there is a big difference between using the book to do this, and using it to tell others who they are: the latter is in fact to abuse others. The intention of the book is the exact opposite of that.

Rickie Hilder
Sydney, Australia
December, 1999

CHAPTER 1
CHILDREN ARE THE FUTURE

The Millenium is upon us, and the world is changing at a rapid rate. Every day there is new information and new technology, with new experiences unfolding, and our lives gather momentum to keep abreast of what is happening. Children are inheriting a far different world. On television and in the media we see many changes around us, with dissolution and the crumbling of the world we knew. Children are resorting to drugs or violence, as they despair, lose hope for themselves and their future, and believe there is no other resolution. They cannot live up to certain expectations, or are depressed because they believe there is more to life than they can foresee for themselves.

Children are our hope for the future. Children are the future. How do we create a world that is safe for the children to live in? How do we ascertain their future and their ability to deal with the stress of so many changes, and provide them with a strong sense of what is valuable to sustain them? How do we let them know they are cherished, and instil hope? How will children combine the values and traditions of history and not make the same mistakes? And what about us? How do adults move with the times, adapt, and embrace these changes? How do we live rich, meaningful lives with a sense of purpose? Do you believe you are fulfilling your life's purpose right now? Have you thought about your life's purpose? Do you think there is more to your life than what's happening now? Do you feel pressure or stress, or that there is more to life than you can foresee for yourself?

READING THIS BOOK COULD BE THE FIRST STEP TO A DIFFERENT LIFE FOR YOU OR YOUR CHILD.

This book is for adults, be they parents, friends, teachers, relatives, carers, or counsellors - but adults who care about children. It is for those who care about their own individuality and that of children, and aspire for themselves and children to be all they can be. It is about building better relationships with children. The information provided can also enhance the understanding of others in your life, whether they are partners, family, business associates, friends, or clients - there is a child within everyone. The one thing we all have in common is that we were children once. The chapters that follow in this book give insights into what is behind our own and children's behavior, and how children adapt and separate from their true selves and potential. It is about enhancing positive feelings of self-concept and self-esteem in children, and upholding them as individuals. Children who are aware of their personal values have a sense of empowerment and their place in the world. I believe that each child matters, that they are unique and special and that there is a reason they come into the world with their own gifts of individuality.

To explore with adults and children our reasons for being in the world, I use colour, word and creativity in simple, gentle and non-confrontational ways. Colour offers keys to patterns of our behaviour. It is a universal language to which we respond. For instance people around the world know the red traffic light means stop, and the green means go. Large corporations spend vast sums of money to determine the impact on the public of colours in staff uniforms, and company logos. What do they want their uniforms, logo, and decor to say about the company? For example blue can mean 'authority' and 'faith', therefore uniforms will be in this colour where 'authority' and 'faith' are part of the message that is meant to be conveyed. The darker the blue, the more the authority and faith. Have you noticed most airline pilots wear dark blue uniforms? I am sure that I would not feel so confident if I noticed the pilot on my flight to Europe sitting in the cockpit in a pink suit. What about you? There is something reassuring when we see the pilot and co-pilot arriving at the airport in those dark blue uniforms. 'Yes, here is someone I can trust who is an authority on flying this plane.' So we are responding to the colours around us every day - and so are children.

Children have rights: The right to be loved. The right to safety. The right to be accepted. The right to kindness. The right to caring. The right to express their truth. The right to peace. The right to their individuality. The right to happiness. The right to a future. The right to get it wrong and make mistakes, as mistakes are a valuable part of our learning and growth. The right to be a child.

Many of these rights are enshrined in the United Nations' Declaration of Children's Rights, yet children don't necessarily experience them.

Children also have needs: The need to be loved. The need for safety. The need to be accepted. The need for kindness. The need for caring. The need to be appreciated. The need to be heard. The need to be valued. The need to be seen. The need for compassion. The need for trust. The need for time. The need for attention. The need to be a child.

As adults we have a special responsibility to preserve the rights of children and to fulfill their needs, or arrange for this to be done. While these rights and needs are common for all children they are expressed in individual and unique ways.

Children remember something that's said to them that is affirming. Can you remember a moment as an adult when something was said to you that made an impact? This is more accentuated when we are a child. Perhaps there is a childhood memory of something that was said to you in the past that made a difference. Now, you can make a difference to yourself, to a child, and to others. You can make a difference. You are here to make a difference. We are created differently, to make a different contribution. There is no other individual quite like you, and your contribution is unique. The point is, the difference we are all here to make in the world, is different for each individual. It is so simple really. Each sees the world through their own perspective, their own lens.

Colours and our individual responses to colours can help us to understand our individuality, our purpose, our uniqueness.

We are like the colours of the rainbow, all different and all beautiful in their own right. Different colours come together to make a rainbow, and yet every colour is quite distinctive. Difference is important in a rainbow. If there was no difference, there could be no rainbow. Each colour of the rainbow has its own story, its own qualities, its own possibilities, its own characteristics, its own potential, its own challenges, and its own gifts. Then when these colours come together, they harmonize and create something impressive that lights up the sky. As individuals, some relate to the colour blue, some to green, some to red, etc. Making your individual choices, and using the information that relates to each colour contained in the following chapters can help you gain a deeper insight into children and yourself.

Children can grow up believing that in order to be loved they have to do something, or behave or look a certain way, live in a given area, be a particular sex, or have a specific education, job, or car; or that they have to like a certain type of activity, sport, food, or music, in order to fit in and be of value. They can spend their lives looking for something outside themselves, when it is inside all the time. Do you find that often you are too hard on yourself? Do you expect yourself to be perfect, the ideal wife, friend, father, mother, grandparent, child, teacher, employee, or employer? You are perfect as you are right now. When we realize this, we are free to make choices about our behaviour and our life, and not keep striving to meet unreal expectation and stress out.

We are born with our value, with our authenticity, with our individuality, with our own true colours. This is who we are, and we do not need to be more than this, or hide this, or try to be something else, in order to be accepted and loved. When we learn that we are okay as we are with all our imperfections, then we no longer need to hide them from other people or ourselves. When we can accept others and ourselves as we are, for who we are, and decide how we want to live our life in line with our values, then we are on the way to realizing our maximum potential. We can blossom and radiate our true colours.

I want every person who reads this book to know that they are here for a reason, that their existence has meaning, that they matter, and that they deserve to be loved exactly the way they are with all their faults. There is a place for you, and a space for you. You are precious and valuable, and you are enough just the way you are. This is the truth. You have your true colours to shine into the world, every one of us does.

Do you feel appreciated for who you really are? Do you feel sure of who you really are? Do you believe there is a part inside you that is waiting to come alive and be revealed? Do you sense that there could be more to your life, more to express more to contribute? Do you ask, 'Who am I and what am I here for?', 'What can I do about it?', 'What are my true colours?', 'Who is this unique individual who is my child?', 'How can I find out more about my children?' This book explores ways of suggesting answers to these questions. What can we do for children, and for ourselves? This book suggests that we can learn something new and offer that to our children. We can offer ourselves compassion for what we did not know before this moment, accept that we did the best we knew at the time, and choose another way of relating to ourselves and to children. We can respect both ourselves and them for who they are and their individuality, and support them to live their true colours.

The purpose of this book is not to mend you or the children. There is nothing to mend, because there is nothing wrong with you or the children. The purpose of the book is to bring awareness and options, so that people can make new choices around how they want to respond in their lives, so they can begin to live the life they were born to have, become what they were born to be and contribute that to the community, and encourage others to do the same. This is important, especially for children and, in turn, their children. The purpose of this book is so that we can create a situation where each individual child matters, and in which they can grow and develop in a world that appreciates their uniqueness. And this begins with adults.

As parents and individuals the best thing we can do for others in our lives, is to get a sense of who we are, our true colours, and live that. This in itself will pass something on, not only to our children, but also to our colleagues, family, friends, and business associates, in our relationships, and as part of our expression in the world. It means that by showing love, compassion and respect to yourself, you will become an example and someone others can learn from. If you can do it, they can do it too. You can become the powerful being you are. Your enthusiasm can be revitalized and you could have a new sense of yourself, with marked differences in how you perceive the world and yourself in it. I have seen adults and children wake up, as if from a sleep, and their aliveness is apparent for all to see. And with children it is so easy. This has been my experience. It is as if they already know and they were waiting for someone to confirm it for them, to validate it. 'I am valuable and worthwhile, I matter, and I can do it': 'I am valuable and therefore everyone else is valuable.'

When children are accepted and loved for themselves, and the world welcomes and receives them as they truly are, it can totally change the life of a child, its future, and the future of those around it. The life of a child is worth this. Your life is worth this. It is as simple as that. You are worth the time it takes. You are worth the time it took me to write this book. If you can make one new choice, take one step towards self-fulfillment and a richer and fuller life, giving to those around you, then my purpose is complete. Whoever and wherever you are, if you were born that makes you valuable. That is my message, and if you believe that about yourself, then your child and others will certainly come to learn it just by being with you. If you can love and accept yourself and risk sharing that in an honest way, if you can give all that you are to the world around you, then the world will be a richer place because you were born. You were born the way you are for a reason. I don't know the reason, but deep in your heart you do. Find out what it is. Take the simple steps in this book. Follow the suggestions in the following pages and teach it to the children. Use the information and insights provided in these chapters to inspire you. Listen, listen to the children, listen to the child within yourself, and you will hear your own music, see your own special colours and shine the light of those into the world.

It is time to re-think for ourselves what our values are. Children know! I have found this in the work I do with them. Children are not blind. They can see what is valuable in the world around them, and they can see with the added perspective of new eyes. They have their own ideas to add to the old. It is allowing and encouraging them to use those ideas they have, those values they have, those gifts they have, that energy they have, in positive, meaningful ways. Children are the future of the world. They need to understand that they have the right to express their truth, and to conduct their lives with meaning: to have a meaningful life. Whatever the child considers meaningful can add meaning to your life. Work with children and guide them step by step through the Values Programme that I have illustrated for you, to establish what they want to create with their lives.

In the past and even at present, many girls have learned to believe they have to be a certain way to attract a husband because they have a message that to be married by a certain age is what life is all about. They will then be seen as successful in the eyes of their girlfriends who have also received this message. What if this does not happen? When this does not happen and they have a different experience from the messages they were given, the individual feels they have failed in some way.

By the same token, many boys are given enormous levels of stress to provide girls with a lifestyle that the girls have learned to believe is appropriate. To sustain this lifestyle the boys believe they need to work in a job that is secure and gives them a reliable income, often without regard to the needs of the individual. Many men work all day trying to keep up with an ever-increasing workload. Then they get home late, then its back to work again on a job that perhaps, if the truth were seen, is meaningless to them. Sometimes it is not possible to admit even to ourselves that we are doing something that has no value to us, because the truth of this would be so confronting. We can be led to believe we have no choices, that we are powerless, and that we have to do this or that. Here is a reason why these days so many children and young adults are rebelling. Some of these beliefs are not adding to their lives. They see the life their parents have led, and it does not fit with their own values or the way they wish to contribute to society and conduct their lives.

Children are not responsible for the unfulfilled ambitions and dreams of their parents or grandparents, but have the right to their individuality and the expression of their uniqueness. This can be an unusual concept for those who have been taught to believe that the family is more important than the individual. Each individual is entitled to their likes and dislikes, and often we don't know what we really like because we haven't realised that we have the right to our likes and dislikes. We believe we should like something because we have been told it is 'right'. The right kind of husband, the right kind of wife, the right kind of job, the right kind of clothes, the right degree, the right friends, the right music, the right haircut, the right look, the right education, the right club, the right age, the right school, the right university, the right behaviour. In some circles, a person's value depends on these 'right' things. However, the truth is, a child is 'right', and has value because it was born. You don't have to do anything to be of value, you are already valuable. Children can have a different haircut, choice of job, wear different clothes, like a different kind of music, be interested in different subjects, have different thoughts, and still hold many traditional values dear to their heart. There is always scope for traditional values, and for these to be expressed by the individual along with newer ideas they may have.

World famous people like Albert Einstein, William Shakespeare, Mother Theresa, Leonardo di Vinci, Mahatma Gandhi, or George Washington had values, and as well they all thought differently, and contributed to the world by their expression of their individuality. They were certainly different and each made a unique contribution. Everyone has something to give: a taxi driver, a nurse, an office worker, a garbage collector, a housewife, a waiter, a student, a child: all are valuable and should be valued. The contributions of every individual are important. Whether these contributions are seen in the eyes of another as great or small, they are important as the expression of the uniqueness of that person and that child. We cannot judge another's value. That is like judging one colour of the rainbow as better than another. Without all the colours, there would be no rainbow. Without difference there would be no rainbow.

Children need to learn that they are not their role, job, clothes, figure, hair, husband, home, wife, or car. They need to learn that their value does not lie with what they do, or what they achieve, or where they live, or what they have, or their education, or whether they are married or not. Their value is because they were born as individuals: their value lies in their individuality and uniqueness. If we were meant to be all the same, we would have been created that way. We are created as individuals because that is what we have to offer to each other and the world, our difference. Not our sameness. We are the colours of the rainbow.

I talk to children about being different, and that we are meant to be different. I tell them it takes many stars to light the sky and they may all look the same, but they are different and shine in their own special way. Every child is like a star, and each has equal value. No star is more valuable than another; they are all stars, and all precious. Each child is a starchild. They are all valuable, and meant to radiate their own individual light, the light they were born with. We all have our own star to radiate, our gifts to give, our way of seeing the world, and in this way, we are all special.

How then do we come together in harmony so that every light can shine equally? By realizing that everyone has a light to shine, and appreciating that difference is important: by appreciating others and wondering what their starlight can reveal to me: 'How can I see more because of the light this star shines?' What values can their light reveal that could be important to me, and help light my way in the world?' 'What can their light show me about my potential, my possibilities, myself?'

Nothing is more valuable than our children, and their sense of their own worth. Children know what they like. They know what they want as their values in their lives. The following chapters will guide you through the various possibilities that are revealed within each colour selection, and you can interpret and gain insights from the colours selected by yourself, and the children around you with whom you work and play.

CHAPTER 2
PATTERNS

Everyone of us, as a human being, was born with our true colours, our original identity, and the core of what we have to offer and contribute. Our characteristics, our gifts, our qualities, our possibilities, our uniqueness, our potential, our authenticity and sense of self is held deep within us like a blueprint, a pattern, a map of our world. This is overlain early in childhood by a different map, a different script, the situation of the family into which we as a child are born and educated. As children we are expected to fit into this preferred script, or we have failed in some way. This preference is what many children become. They learn to believe they should follow certain paths to be 'right'. This is the right script, this is the right map, this is the path you should take, the way you should be: it is the right pathway to be a boy, the right pathway to be a girl, the right way to be a man, a woman, a father, mother, a success. 'Follow this map.' 'Follow this script.' 'This is our script, and you need to use it if you want to get anywhere in the world.' It is this script or map that has been the way for adults, the parents, and they want to pass on this information. Because of this, many expectations are put on children.

The child's own map, their blueprint, which contains their pattern of thoughts, feelings, qualities, characteristics and contributions, is not always considered important enough: 'What would a child know?' is often an adult attitude. When this happens, how can a child then believe in itself, and the value of what it has to offer? 'Will I be accepted if I have a different point of view?' 'Will I be good enough?' 'Will what I say make any difference?' 'It's best not to say what I really think. I'd better not reveal my true colours.' These are some of the doubts and fears that confront the child. To complicate matters, there can be varying scripts at school and college, as well as within sporting, social and recreational groups. The child can be subject to multiple scripts that often may be conflicting.

Their fear of being different and criticised prevents most children from learning to trust their inner wisdom and their inner guidance, and they go along with the imposed script, along with the crowd. They learn to believe that 'different' equals 'wrong'. They learn to conform rather than question. They spend their lives trying to follow another's script, trying to be something else, another colour, and this has unfortunate implications and consequences. If we are trying to be something we are not, we cannot be successful at it, because we are not it. How can green be violet? How can blue be red? Furthermore we miss the opportunity of living our true colours and contributing all this means to the world. It is enormously stressful trying to live up to another's expectations. It is actually far easier to be ourselves, rather than trying to be something that pleases others. It is easier to live our own map of the world, rather than the map of another. We were born with our map, our pattern, our blueprint. It is inherent in us.

If we accept that we are all born with our own blueprint then we can ask, 'What are my true colours?' 'What are the true colours of the children with whom I am associated?' 'What is in my pattern, and how do I ensure my blueprint, my map of the world comes alive in my life?' 'How do I live according to what I consider valuable?' We will discuss ways to work step by step to find answers to such questions.

So the map of the world that is taught to the child is like a script which creates a set of beliefs and perceptions about the world, and them in it. How is the world going to treat them? Will they be accepted? Will they be listened to? Will they matter? Will they have to struggle to survive? Will they be successful? Will they be good enough? Will they fail? Will they find love? Will money always be an issue with them? Does one parent give them messages that create a script about money and imply you have to work hard and put in long hours for it; while the other parent gives script messages that imply 'don't worry, spend, spend, spend?' Script messages are given to the child non-verbally as well. Does the child's learnt script say a man has to work hard and have little time with his family, that his needs and skills come second to being seen as successful and a good provider? What qualifies as success in this script? Is the girl meant to get married and have children by a certain age? Is the girl meant to have a job to fill in time till she gets married, or can she have a career? What does this script say about a girl's individuality? Can she contribute to society in another way? Does she feel guilty if she does? Does she feel content?

Certain learnt scripts have a message that when a girl marries, her husband will be like a hero who solves all her problems, and they will live happily ever after like the fairy tales and romantic novels. What if this does not happen? Or what of a script that says 'When I get my degree all my troubles will be over, and getting a good job will be easy.' What if this is not your experience? Another script says, 'To be successful you should be part of the company, then you will be somebody and look important, because the company is successful and knows where it is going.' What if you don't want to follow this path. Do you then believe you are unsuccessful, unimportant, and nobody? We can be taught to believe that our identity and value is connected to our work or our behaviour, and many scripts say this. If I do this, I am somebody and valuable. When the truth is, we are somebody and valuable just as we are.

Has the child incorporated a message into their learned script that says 'you are not wanted?' This may not be spoken, but the child knows. Does the child feel unwanted because they were conceived by mistake? Is this child the one that parents did not want to have so soon after the child born before it, or is it the one born too late after the child born before it?: 'We don't want children right now.' 'We're too young to have children.' 'We are too old to have children.' 'We only wanted one child....we only wanted two'. 'We wanted a boy.' 'We don't want children at all, there is no money, there is no room.' Is this child angry because it had to grow up quickly as there were other babies soon after, and it didn't have a childhood like it saw the other/s having? Is one child compared to another? Is the third child not as special with the mother or father as the other two children who already have their place, or does this child take the special place in the affection of the mother or father replacing another? Sometimes the second child can feel second best. How does this feel for a child? What can the child do with these true feelings? Instead of just expressing them and moving on, they can be unexpressed and come out in other ways, especially if the child's imposed and learned script says that having feelings is not okay.

Many learned scripts expect perfection. Nobody is perfect, we all make mistakes, and we are all human. To try to be super human and perfect, or expect perfection from a child, yourself, or another, is a set up to fail because we are all human beings and all fallible. A mistake can include showing a feeling, if feelings were not allowed or not accepted. Some scripts say that feeling sensitive, or showing anger or fear can be equated with weakness, so we cut ourselves off from these feelings and our humanness. Some people believe they don't deserve to feel happiness and joy. Without feelings a child cannot experience total aliveness

It is a part of life to learn and grow. Learning, by definition, means that we don't know, so to expect our children and ourselves to know what we don't know, makes life extremely difficult. To shame a child by expecting them to get it right the first time and never make a mistake, sets up behaviour where they have to look like they know everything and can't show their human fallibility, and humility. We are all fallible as human beings. We can learn to believe as children that we are not okay when we make a mistake; many scripts say this. This puts children and adults under enormous stress not to make a mistake, or not to be seen to be making mistakes, or they experience intense shame.

Children respond very well to examples that use their heroes, and I often use examples of famous sporting identities to illustrate a point I want to make. For instance there is a world famous basketball player called Michael Jordan who is highly skilled at making successful shots with the basketball. I ask the children to think about how many times Michael Jordan would have had to throw the ball and practice before he gained this skill. If he thought he was a failure because of all his missed shots, he would not have persevered and become arguably the best basketball player in the world. He learned how to make the big shots, because he used his 'mistakes' to see what did not work. By correcting these 'mistakes', he learned how to make the winning shots. So he used his mistakes to learn how to achieve what he wanted. We too can think about our mistakes as part of learning, and not see them as failures. We can see obstacles as gifts, as learning experiences that re-enforce our knowledge and ability to carry out what we want, and are here to do. We can add this to our script. If the focus is placed on failure and the child is shamed, it leads to children who grow into adults who are too ashamed to try in case they fail, and this becomes their script.

Do the children in the family behave in a certain way with the mother and change when the father comes home? Does the environment, and so the script, contain love and acceptance, or fear. For example, does it include 'Fear I'll get it wrong,' 'fear I won't know enough,' 'fear I'll make a mistake,' 'fear I have to be a certain way and I must be sure to behave this way or my parents won't accept me'? Some adults still revert to childhood behaviour when they visit or talk to their parents or family. I am not saying this is wrong. What I am saying is, this is our behaviour, and our behaviour is what we learn to do. Our behaviour is not who we are. We are not our behaviour. We are more than our behaviour. Our behaviour is something we can make choices about at any time in our lives, based on new information and awareness as we learn and grow, and we can pass this on to children. There is a difference between behaviour based on respect, and behaviour based on fear. We can change our learned script and our behaviour at any time.

A child can feel neglected because they do not get the time and attention they need, and their learnt script says that they are less important than whatever does get the time and attention. For example, they can feel less important than another child, than the work of their father, than what it is that keeps their mother too busy to attend to them, than the other women in the life of their father who is too preoccupied to come home and spend time with them, than the sickness of the mother, or than the needs of the mother that the child is expected to fulfil because the father is absent. There are many situations where a child experiences 'less than', and I've given just a few examples. It is reasonable for a child to have thoughts and feelings about these situations. Often they are unable to express these feelings, which subsequently get locked in, and can carry over into adulthood. Then because their learnt script says they come from a 'less than' position in their lives, many adults can feel inadequate in friendships, relationships, in social situations, and at work. Often they then try to compensate by acting 'more than', with unpleasant consequences.

When people have the opportunity to express feelings held from childhood situations, there can be an immense relief. It is as though they drop a burden that they have been carrying all their lives. Because it takes energy to repress these feelings and block them from our consciousness, having the feelings and expressing them actually gives the individual more energy, clearing the way to freedom, healing, growth and aliveness.

It can be challenging when we realize that we have been part of a system which created these situations for us, and then we have unknowingly, and certainly unintentionally, passed the script on because we didn't know any better at the time. I would suggest that in the past, you did the best you could do. You did what you did, because that was all you knew then. You cannot do more than that. It is not possible to do what we do not yet know. There are no college degrees on how to raise children. Parents do not wake up each morning and think 'How can I neglect my child today?' or 'How can I suppress my child's spirit?' or 'How can I put stress and pressure on my child?' We want the best for our children, as our parents wanted the best for us. Often as parents learn more information, they feel concern at their previous misguided efforts with children. If this is the case for you, perhaps you need to remember that every day is a new day and a new opportunity.

For myself, as time has passed and I've learnt more, I've felt upset to realise the mistakes I've made as a friend, and as a parent, particularly as a parent. I wanted the best for my child, nevertheless I made mistakes. I have had regrets during the course of my life, as I've studied and gained knowledge, some of which is contained in this book. Part of me wished it was possible to have the opportunity of going back into the past, and doing it over again with the benefit of my new knowledge, the benefit of hindsight. This is not possible, and I needed to remember I made the best decisions I could at the time. At times it was a painful experience, and part of the process of my learning and growth has been to feel the pain, rather than avoid it. Feelings have a beginning, a middle, and an end, and do not last forever, and every feeling has a gift. It is important to remember that all feelings are gifts that have been given to us for a reason. If we were not meant to have them, we would not have been given them. They are part of us. The gift of pain is growth. Over time I am learning to be compassionate to myself and accept I will make mistakes as a parent and as a person. I need to remember that every day is a new day and a new opportunity.

I suggest you have your feelings about what has been in your life. Maybe you have an inner loneliness, maybe frustration, or grief, or resentment that time has passed and you have not been able to live your true colours. Perhaps you have not lived in accordance with your values. or may feel sad, angry, ashamed, sorry, guilty, confused, lost, anxious or whatever. Allow yourself to have and express the feeling. It is just a feeling. Then you can use that released energy to move, and behave the way you choose from now on, based on knowledge you've gained. Please do not use new information to try and get everything right, expecting yourself to be the perfect mother, father, parent, grandparent, husband, wife, teacher, counseller, or friend; the perfect anything. Trying to be perfect, as I have already suggested, can set us up to fail, because we all make mistakes, we are human. Use information to make choices, not judgements. We have the right to our problems, a fact some people find hard to accept. Problems are a normal part of life.

Knowledge can bring a new dawning, and an opportunity to re-evaluate life and learn to live again. Sometimes we can resist change and cling to past behaviour even if that is uncomfortable because it is what we know and it is familiar. One of the reasons for this is if we let go of what we know, we have to enter the unknown. It is normal to feel apprehensive at the point of change and the unknown. In actual fact, all our tomorrows are unknown, and we are dealing with it on some level all our lives. Children deal with it every day, as they learn, grow, and open up to make the unknown known. As adults we are continually facing the unknown as we transform with natural completions and evolutions. We complete our childhood, and move into our teens. Then we move into our twenties, and maybe get a job, maybe many different jobs in our lives. Maybe we move into relationships, maybe many. The possibilities for change and the unknown are manifold. It is a part of life to learn and grow and face the unknown.

So learned scripts set up patterns of behaviour in children, and this behaviour is what we do. It is not who we are. These imposed scripts and patterns are set up in various ways, as we learn to adapt, fit in, and be 'right', and all this takes us away from our authentic self, until we can wonder who we really are. Children from an early age get taught a script, a map of the world of how they should be. And all the time, their authenticity is being covered. Children need their authenticity and their difference, the difference they were created with, so they can fulfil their lives. They need to express their true colours, and fulfil their blueprint by contributing this to the community.

If children are not encouraged to express their individuality, it has consequences. As adults your past affects your present and causes repeat patterns of behaviour in the future. The reason we look at the past is not to blame, but to uncover and rediscover the authenticity. To recognise, rescue, and restore the true colours. Blame is not an option, nor a solution. There is no point in blaming anyone for what happened in the past. Parents, carers, family, teachers and friends gave what they knew. This is all they could do. Putting energy into blame keeps the individual stuck, when the energy could go into moving on and taking responsibility for where they are now, and where they choose to go from here. They can look at their learnt script and see what they believe is true and what is not. The human response of having thoughts and feelings about the events of our lives, is a very different experience from blaming. Expressing our feelings is validating and freeing, and restores our dignity, whereas blame seeks to take away the dignity of another and keeps us imprisoned. The information in this book is not about blame, or judging yourself or anyone else. Far from it. The information is about creating the world we want for children. It is about choices and individuality and our true colours. It is about caring and sharing. It is about children and adults contributing our individuality, our differences, and our light, because we are important, and valuable, and all our lives have meaning.

So how do we gain insights into different patterns, and the true colours of children and ourselves? I work with children and adults step by step in the following way.

The first step is to choose the colour combination that attracts you the most from over 100 combinations in this book (see the first three pages in the colour section). When making your selection, do not think about it too much. For example, you may choose red over blue, or clear over pink, or pale blue over pale blue. It is a good idea to follow these steps yourself, because your personal experience can give you a sense of how it could be for children. You will have a connection with the steps, rather than describing them from a book. And as well, I would like you to have the gift of personal insights for yourself.

The meanings of the colours chosen are provided in Chapters 5 to 19. The colour on the <u>top</u> of your selection reveals <u>how people see you</u>, what you can experience in your life, what you are working with and learning from, and how you reveal yourself to the world. The <u>bottom</u> of your colour selection shows <u>how you are at the deepest level</u>. It can be more hidden from view. More, it reveals how you would know yourself, it shows your greatest gifts, and what you bring to this life. Together they reveal your potential, your gifts, your qualities, your possibilities, and what you can learn and contribute. They illustrate your true colours.

So now you have made your choice of colours, the next step is to go to the page in this book with the circular pattern on it (see page 74). Using coloured pencils or crayons that match the colours in your selection, colour in this pattern. When I am working with children or adults I give them a photocopy of this pattern, so maybe you would like to do this too. Make as many copies as you wish.

I suggest to participants that they find a space in the room where they feel comfortable, mostly on the floor, and they colour in as I am talking to them. When I have given this to children in a school situation I've found it important that they are not sitting at school desks which can prompt the children to feel they have to get it right. If they sit on the floor they usually feel more relaxed and can absorb what I am saying at the same time. In fact it is remarkable the way children have remembered what I said to them as they colour in this way. Frankly, I have been amazed at the written and taped feedback given by the children to teachers after I have left, some of which was provided in the Preface. They repeat most of what I have said and have assimilated so much information. Ostensibly they are colouring, but they are listening and learning at the same time. They are not under any pressure, and the feedback shows they enjoy my sessions.

I keep it really simple and tell children how they are all special in their own way, and they can colour their patterns in their own way, any way they choose. It is their creativity and it is their choice. Each one of us is creative in our own different way. We have our own way of seeing things, and our own way of doing things, and no one is the same as anyone else, and no way is the right way. Every way is right. I say, with creativity we can't make mistakes, we just change our mind. So colour this pattern in the way that you choose. Whatever is right for you. Everyone is special. And they are colouring as I am talking. You will notice I am repeating the same message in a different manner, because repetition is how we learn, or possibly the child's mind was somewhere else when I said it previously.

And I say we are all creative in our own way, some people are creative in their minds, some with their hands, some with words. And I ask them to be creative and think of words in their mind right now that make them feel happy, or words that make them feel unhappy. And I tell them that words we say can make others feel happy or sad as well. And that we are creating in our minds all the time, just like they are doing now. Are we creating words in our minds that make us feel good, or not? Then I suggest I'd like them to think of a word about themselves that makes them feel very happy, and when they have done that, to find another word that makes them feel even happier. The whole time they are colouring. I talk as I walk around the room and observe what each child is doing. I observe the process they take with the pattern, how they use the colours they have selected, and in what order. It is very significant.

When I am talking to the children I am not merely saying they are different and special, my words are sincere, and I am aware of the tone of my voice, using gentleness and strength. When you take children through this process, I urge you to be mindful of how you speak to them. Children know if you mean what you say, so ensure your voice and words are congruent, and remember 80% of messages are given non-verbally.

When the child has finished and you are talking about their work, firstly always ask what the colours mean to them. Listen while they share their thoughts and feelings, and allow them to tell you what this creative expression represents to them. Observe which colour the child uses the most, and whether this colour is on the top or bottom half of their colour selection.

To gain insights about yourself now that you have taken the step of colouring your pattern with my words in mind, I will pose some questions regarding your method of approaching this task. Please use these questions as guidelines to recognise the many and varied ways of colouring the pattern. You may be surprised at how much can be revealed by this very simple process.

When colouring the pattern, which colour did you use the most? Which colour did you choose to use first, if there were two colours? Did you start from the outside of the pattern, or the inside? Did you do the circle in the middle first? Did you do the outside in one colour all the way around or change? Did you use one colour for a while, and then change? Or did you use the colours alternately? Did you take a path and find your way to the centre? Did you work in circles from the outside in, or the inside out? Did you turn the pattern to the side so you were working horizontally, or was it vertical? Did you start from the inside, and then go to the outside and work back in, or did you work your way from the centre to the outside, then work your way around the outside? Did you start at one side and colour to the centre and then work from there in a line to the other side? Did you colour most, or all one side of the pattern first? Did you start at the top, or the bottom, or the side? Did you notice what prompted you to start where you did? Did you think a lot before you started? Did you think there must be a right way and hesitate, or just start? What were your thoughts as you did the pattern? Did you feel confused, if so what did you do then? Did you stay where you were, or did you move to another spot, or did you change colours? Maybe you did none of these. What did you do? From these questions and their answers you can see there are so many options and possibilities of colouring something that looks very simple. Remember there is no right way. Each child will have their own process working with this, and that is their right as an individual.

That is why I walk around the room as I am talking, to see what each child is doing. I am observing all these possibilities. I am seeking to understand the world from the viewpoint of the child. What is the world through the eyes of this child? Because I have been talking and telling them how different they are and there is no right way, it has set the scene for them to perceive how many ways there are of approaching a given task. About half way through the process, I ask them to walk around the room and see how creative each person is. I have them do this reasonably quickly, so they don't become distracted. At the end when they hold up their completed work and become aware of how different it is for each person, I remind them of what they observed walking around, when the work was in progress. Then they come to appreciate that not only is the end product different, but also the journey to produce it is different. Not only have they learned by hearing me say we are all individuals and have different ways of doing things, they have experienced it as well, in non-confronting ways. It is a visual lesson in how we view situations from an entirely different angle, and see a different point of view.

This leads to the children becoming aware each has the right to their difference, and to appreciate how beautiful the work is that each one has created. I point out that while it is true we have our individual way of doing things, we can also learn and find inspiration from the creativity of others. I tell them they chose their colours to do the pattern, and that, as I have already said, we are like the colours of the rainbow, all different and all beautiful in their own right. Different colours come together to make a rainbow, and yet every colour is quite distinctive. Difference is important in a rainbow. If there was no difference, there could be no rainbow. Each colour of the rainbow is different, but when these colours come together they create something spectacular and beautiful.

At schools they have put the completed patterns on the wall, sometimes laminated, to recognise and uphold the individuality of children in the class. This exercise leaves an imprint on the group of the many ways of seeing and doing the same task, and forms the basis for the step we'll approach in the next chapter. The exercise also has them subtly experience the power of the mind, the power of words, and what we create with what we think and say. There is a belief that being 'creative' means being artistic. I believe our creativity is how we express our individuality, and this is revealed in many ways, not essentially by the artistic process. We can also create our world by the way we think about a situation. Something that would be a disaster to one person is ordinary to another.

The children have the advantage of my speaking to them as they work, bringing an added level to their learning. They are using their sense of hearing, as well as sight and touch, making their process more multi-dimensional than yours would have been working in silence. Clearly, from the way we colour this pattern there is much to learn about how we approach and carry out tasks, the various ways we function, and our individual strengths. From many case studies, I have included a variety to give ideas for different methods of interpretation.

In interpreting patterns, I am considering some of the following questions. When approaching a task is the individual someone who goes right to the heart of it? Do they like to think before making a move, or do they move quickly? Do they relish a challenge? Do they take their time and finish each part of the task before moving on to the next? Are they impatient to get to the end? Are they the persevering type? Are they quick with decisions? Do they like to think of options before taking a step? Do they see tasks in broad sweeps? Do they trust the process and allow themselves time? Do they prefer a variety of tasks at once, or one at a time? Do they like to jump right in? Do they like to attend to details and approach a task one step at a time, and not think about the next step till they come to it? When given a task do they get the overall idea of one section and complete that before moving on?

And what of your reaction to this process. Are you judging what you have done? Are you pleased about seeing more of yourself? How was this process for you? There is no right way, your way is right for you.

There is a further step you can take for personal insights, and it is regarding the questions I posed about your techniques for completing the pattern. I mentioned observations I make on how the children worked, and asked how it was for you. Asking the questions is designed to show various options and possibilities, and give information to the individual. How each individual reacts to the questions also gives them information. You will notice the questions are quite simple and general to begin with, and then what I described were various ways the pattern has been approached.

Did you become confused with the questions? If so, what did you do? Did you leave them and go straight to the end of the section? Did you struggle for a while and then give up trying to work it out? Did you actually colour the pattern, or did you think it was only for children? Did you think it was all too complicated, and that you could not understand? Did you become impatient and frustrated with yourself? Did you lose interest, or keep reading waiting for a mention of the way you coloured the pattern? Did you find it interesting that there are so many ways of colouring the pattern? Did you wonder what the questions revealed about you? Did you think, I'll leave it and come back to it later? Did you come back to it later? Did you feel curious to know more? Did you follow the questions and visualise in your mind what I was saying? Did you use the pattern to follow what I was saying? Maybe you did none of these. What did you do? Remember there is no right way. Everyone is different. You have the absolute right to your own way.

It is useful to follow the different ways the pattern has been approached to experience how it is for another. Following their map is like walking in their shoes, and getting a sense of how the world is through their eyes. It can be a very interesting and enlightening exercise. It takes the understanding that we are all different, to another level. You can learn so much about yourself and others. There is a sense of how much is inside another person, and their uniqueness. It deepens the listening experience, it heightens compassion, and it opens the doors to understanding children and others in a world where they often believe they are not understood. Taking the time to go through their pattern with them, after they have completed it in their own way, shows you are interested and care. It can be enlightening to see how differently you and your children approach the pattern and the colours you use.

We are all different, we are meant to be different.

Before you work with children, I suggest you read through my work with the pattern, from the section beginning with the choosing of the colours, and become clear in your mind what to say to children, and how to approach this situation. This way you will feel more confident. Perhaps you could practise with an adult friend until you feel quite comfortable.

Every one has their own personal method of doing this pattern, and each is special. That is what I tell the children and they can see it for themselves. Choosing the same colours as another does not mean we will create the same pattern. So your colours give insights, your patterns give insights, and together they give a picture of your individuality, your skills, and your gifts.

PATTERN CASE STUDIES

The following case studies, drawn from children and adults with whom I have worked in Australia and overseas, are included to illustrate a variety of patterns and how they relate to the individual. In total there are 4 patterns included. You will find them in the colour section of the book. They are numbered 1-4.

There is one pattern and case study given in detail (1). The next two patterns (2.3) feature the colour red combined with two different colours. I have included these two because they reveal the characteristics of individuals using red, and indicate the influence of the other colour contained in the combination. The next pattern (4) features the colours turquoise and magenta.

Details of the meaning of colours commented on here are discussed fully in Chapters 5 to 19.

The names used in all case studies in this book are fictitious and some details of the cases and contexts have been changed to preserve the anonymity of participants.

The reason I used the case study of Takako from Japan in Case Study 1, is to say that she could not change the life situation of the two children, Kanji and Emi; that was not possible for her to do. What she could do, however, was to use the pattern to give them a sense of their worth by telling them they were special in their own way. Takako encouraged them to express themselves, and listened to them as they talked when doing the pattern. She made a difference in the way that was possible. If she can do it, so can you. You too, can make the difference to a child.

CASE STUDY 1

At the end of each workshop where I expand the information given in this book, I give each student a copy of the pattern to photocopy and use where they believe it is appropriate. Six months after taking the workshop, Takako, a student in Japan showed me the following case study where she gave the pattern to Kanji, a five year old boy. Takako said she asked Kanji to choose two colours from crayons and he selected violet and green. His three-year old sister, Emi chose violet and gold and I have included her case study in the next chapter on the Startree.

As Takako described it, the parents of these two children own a sushi bar, and they are too busy to attend to the children. Their father Yuji started the sushi bar and at first hired staff. According to Takako because he is so aggressive and rude, the staff would always leave, so Yuji said his wife Risa must work at the sushi bar with him. This meant that the two children Emi and Kanji must also come to the sushi bar and spend all day there and into the night. They were confined to a space less than the size of a tatami mat (roughly the size of a bath towel), with nothing to occupy them except one video. Yuji and Risa do not speak to them and they had to be quiet, and not disturb their parents or the customers.

Kanji kept disappearing out of the shop and did not want to come back. Emi said that she is tired all the time. Takako said that as Kanji did the pattern, many times he asked her 'is this okay?' He wanted to know if he was doing the pattern the right way, and did not want to make mistakes and get into trouble. Kanji had chosen violet where one of the issues is trying to be perfect, and wondering if what they do will be good enough. While Kanji was colouring the pattern his mother Risa was saying violet is an awful colour and why didn't he use another colour which she liked. She was criticizing his work as he was colouring.

Kanji really wanted to know that what he was doing was okay, because he had learned that whatever he did was wrong or not perfect, so he kept disappearing from the sushi bar. Violet children often feel different and somehow wrong in their difference. Kanji had chosen green, and one of the issues for green is space and freedom, and this would perhaps be part of the reason why he was running away from the confinement of a small space less than the size of a tatami mat. Green also reveals a kind and generous heart, and Yuji, Kanji's father, who considered kindness was weakness, did not appreciate this. Notice how the violet seems to predominate in Kanji's pattern, and the green either threads through, or is in pockets, as if trying to find enough space.

Green also suggests a lack of time, attention and direction. And the neglect a child can feel because it compares itself to whatever is getting the time and attention of the parents. For Kanji, his learnt script suggested that he was less important than the work of the parents, as all day and into the night he is confined to silence in a tiny area. So he ran away. He also had the belief that he is not good enough, as revealed by the way that he spoke while doing the pattern. Kanji will likely carry this sense of himself into adulthood.

As Kanji was doing the pattern and asking if it was okay, Takako was saying that each child is different, and that we are meant to be different, and that each child is special, in the way I have suggested in this chapter. The little boy was so pleased with his work, that he put his name on the back, and wanted to have the pattern placed on the wall.

This case study reveals that using this simple pattern technique offers the opportunity to teach children self-worth and that they are valuable as they are. It is a subtle method of building self-confidence and self esteem, and every child deserves this.

CASE STUDY 2

Joseph chose red/deep magenta, and his pattern started in the centre with deep magenta. He worked with this colour while the red pencil was held in his other hand at the ready.

He approached the task very rapidly, switching pencils, with little attention to detail, as his focus was on movement and action. These are red qualities. You will notice that as soon as he had the idea of the pattern, Joseph coloured the outside red sections in a single sweep.

Joseph can get very frustrated when he is not active, and needs to be involved in physical activity, such as sports. He is not interested at all in studying at school. However, he is a keen sportsman who likes to train, and put these skills into practice. Joseph enjoys studying the tactics of opponents, and gets satisfaction from analyzing the games and utilizing this knowledge to win - possibilities found in deep magenta. Joseph has a way of motivating others in his team and seems to bring out the best in them.

Often individuals who choose deep magenta are interested in delving into the hidden, and understanding what is behind the surface. They are not easily fooled. They can be great motivators as they recognise abilities in people that are not obvious to those individuals.

Joseph has the tendency to be disruptive in class as he is not interested in school subjects and wants to be either spending time studying sport or actively engaged in doing something physical. Because he has not given any attention to his studies he has not done well, and has been shamed because of his poor results. Red, which is also hidden in deep/magenta, holds the possibility for shame.

Perhaps instead of constantly telling Joseph to keep still and chastising him for his need to be active, he could be given activities which require his determination and endurance, attributes found in red. Deep magenta individuals can be misunderstood, and often they cannot see their own potential whilst seeing so much in others. In Joseph's case I suggested finding a subject that does interest him, even a little, something which would require investigation, something where he would need to delve and use the skills found in deep magenta.

One of the challenges for Joseph is that the red aspect of him is an extrovert, whilst the deep magenta part is content remaining in the background, and contributing by working behind the scenes. He needs to have an interest which would motivate him to contribute the attributes of both colours.

CASE STUDY 3

Julie, a woman in her early thirties, started this red/blue pattern in a hurry with red at the top, and quickly moved to the centre, then across to the other side in almost the same way. You will notice the red loops at the top of the pattern are not coloured individually, they are coloured in sections.

Then Julie changed to blue and started first with the outline, going more slowly. The way she worked changed completely when she changed colours. Blue has a more calm thoughtful approach, completing work in a serene fashion. A person choosing this colour combination has the possibility of characteristics which are seemingly incompatible.

Julie laughed and said the description fitted her to a T, when I interpreted the work and suggested that the colours used, combined with the way the pattern was approached, could show a likelihood of someone who rushed headlong into things before thinking, and then thought about it when they were already involved. Also there would be the likelihood of someone who finished tasks before other people, and then could become impatient with others for being so slow.

Julie said she noticed that she had already completed the red part of the pattern when others in the group were still scratching the surface of the task. Julie said the impulsive part of her gets frustrated when others are so slow around her. Red people can tend to work in bursts, and really get things done. Frequently they have burnout and need to recoup their energy before moving on to something new. Julie said these aspects of red described her.

Julie was struggling with balancing her blue characteristics, of someone who wants a peaceful life that is calm and tranquil, with the more adventuresome qualities of red. She said she could not put these two parts of herself together, and frequently seemed at odds with herself. This was exemplified in the pattern where Julie said it needed the white spaces in between the two colours, as without the white, the red and blue 'didn't fit'.

Julie's learnt script said that women should be quiet and docile and take a back seat, and she really resented this. She was told she was 'too much', and 'over the top', and 'hard to handle', and felt shame about this outgoing aspect of herself – all possibilities found in red. Julie has struggled with the blue issues of trust, and would rather do everything herself than trust others, so is frequently exhausted and angry – found in red.

Seeing herself through the pattern and colours was very important for Julie, and she said it enabled her to understand herself more. All of her life she had thought she was complicated and that there was something wrong with her, now she could see a way to combine the characteristics and express these in a productive way.

In fact by the time we had discussed each participant's pattern individually in the group, Julie had digested the information from her pattern's interpretation. She had decided that she could now colour the white spaces in her pattern, and complete it in red and blue, something she could not do at first. Julie had recognised her gifts, and could bring seemingly conflicting aspects of her personality into a constructive, integrated whole.

CASE STUDY 4

Angela, a woman in her twenties, chose turquoise/magenta. She started with a magenta dot in the centre and then coloured all the magenta that you see in the pattern, before she began using the turquoise. In fact all the white spaces in this pattern were to be coloured in turquoise. So although she began with magenta, the majority of the pattern when finished, would have been in turquoise.

It is interesting because turquoise can indicate someone who is shy and reserved, and often expresses themselves through artistic pursuits. They can be progressive and seen by others as unusual, and Angela said all these qualities apply to her.

Magenta children often experience a sense of abandonment, and as adults look for someone to love who will fill the emptiness. Angela said she really related to this in her life. You will notice when she did her pattern that most of the loops coloured in magenta are in pairs. And that when she began to colour with turquoise, she put it beside a loop that was already filled with magenta. So far there is no turquoise loop in the pattern sitting by itself.

Angela expressed wanting to be with people, but not knowing how to do this, so she is looking everywhere for love, or the 'right person', someone she can be close to, so she won't feel so alone and unloved. She is looking for her fantasy prince, an issue found in turquoise. In her own way she expressed this in the pattern, by moving all over it pairing loops with the loving caring colour of magenta, and then intending to complete the fantasy with turquoise.

Angela worked the pattern in an entirely unique fashion, and has an unusual creative style which reveals initiative and a variety of talents. She has the ability to see the big picture.

These four Case Studies indicate how the pattern, combined with the colours, gives insights into the individual, and their gifts and possibilities. After the children have completed their patterns I then work with ways that children can be encouraged and supported to contribute productively their gifts and values to the community, through the Values Programme. This is the focus of the next chapter.

THE PATTERN

CHAPTER 3
THE STARCHILD

THE VALUES PROGRAMME

This is where we discuss how to work with children's values, and their map of the world both individually and in group situations. It is where they can be given a sense that they are unique, cherished, and valued. It is where they have the opportunity of deepening the understanding we touched upon with the patterns, regarding appreciating their difference and that of others. It is where their contribution is fostered, nurtured, and encouraged. It is where they learn about values and become aware of their own. It is where they learn that what they say and think matters. It is where they experience openness, tolerance and celebration of their individuality. Its where I talk to hem about being different, that we are meant to be different, and there is no other individual quite like them.

THE STARTREE

I tell children that it takes many stars to light the sky and they may all look the same, but they are different and shine in their own special way. No star is more valuable than another. They are all stars and all precious. Every child is like a star, and each has equal value. Each one of them is a Starchild. They are all valuable and meant to shine the light they were born with, their starlight. We all have our own star to radiate, our gifts to give, our way of seeing the world, and in this way we are all special. We saw from creating our patterns how different we are, how each child was creative in their own way, and that we could learn from each other. We saw there is not one right way. We saw there are many ways, many different viewpoints. So how do we come together in harmony with every light shining equally? It is by realizing that everyone is a Starchild, and has a light to shine, and appreciating that difference is important: by appreciating and respecting others, and wondering what their starlight can reveal.

I describe to the children how with our creativity we can create with words, how words can make us feel, how we become aware that there are words in our mind, and we are creating with those words even when we are doing something else. I talk about the way these words can make us feel happy or sad. I then ask them, 'So what do you want to create with your words?' 'Which words do you think are important?' Then I hold up the Startree, which you will find illustrated on page 96. Please feel free to photocopy it and use it in your work with children. I say to the children: 'You are a Starchild, this is your Startree and these stars are growing on your tree.' 'What words do you want to grow on these stars?' 'Which Starwords would you like to grow with your friends and in your classroom?' Which Starwords would you like to have in your school and at home?' 'Which words are special to you?' I then give them some examples of words and they can choose any of these words, or none of them. I say things like:

'Take your time to think what you want in your life, the Starwords you want to grow.' 'Anything you want, it is your choice.' 'Do you want 'friendship', or 'kindness' or 'trust', or perhaps 'harmony', or 'acceptance', or 'courage'?' 'If you think one of those creative words is right for you, put that on a star on your Startree.' 'You can go slowly if you want time to think.' 'Take your time, there is no need to rush.' 'Which words are coming into your mind that you believe are valuable and important to have at your school and at home?' 'It is your Startree, and your creativity, and you can create anything you want.' 'What do you think is important?' 'What do you value?' 'You may value, 'self-confidence', or 'honesty', or 'fun,' or 'fairness'.' 'And you can change a word on your Startree at any time if you decide something is more important to you.'

I suggest that you always keep it simple when you talk to the children, using age-related language without talking down to them, and remember to repeat the messages in various ways. The Programme is in the guise of creativity, not study, even though the subject is reasonably serious. It is a creative learning process, simple, and enjoyable. Children can learn and have fun at the same time. When you feel it necessary you could give a short, simple and direct explanation as you name some values. Don't talk all the time, give them the space to think for themselves. When they seem stuck, offer suggestions. I have given suggestions for you to offer (see page 95). There are subtle differences in some of these values to cater for what appeals to the age, educational level, and individuality of the children. Talk slowly as you walk around the room observing the children's work, giving them the sense that you are there for them, and are interested in what they do. They will know when you are.

I say to the children, 'perhaps in your life you think that 'love' is valuable, and you would like to see 'love' growing on your Startree...Maybe 'care for the environment', or 'understanding', or 'co-operation', are important to you....Or 'sincerity', or 'forgiveness', or 'patience'. 'What do you want to shine in your life?' 'What starlight do you want to shine from your Startree?' 'What do you think is valuable, what do you choose to grow on your Startree?' 'Everyone is different and everyone decides what he or she wants to create.' 'Maybe you can learn something you would like on your tree by looking at another person's values'. 'Remember how much we can learn from one another'.

When the children have completed their Startree they can colour it if they wish. You can gain insights into their choice of colours, from the following chapters. You may be surprised at the depth of the child's perceptions and how traditional many of their values are. I have included examples of Startrees from individuals of various ages, to illustrate how they want to create their map of the world.

CREATING A GROUP STARTREE

When working with a group, whether in a classroom situation or privately, once the children have had the experience of creating their own Startree, you can take the Programme to another level and invite them to make suggestions for their group Startree. This is where they get to experience interdependence, co-operation, respect and the power of relationship. This is where they experience it is okay to make mistakes. This is where they learn they can use their failures to learn and achieve even more. This is where they have a group experience to express freedom of choice. It sets up the belief that no matter what the circumstances of our life are, we are free to choose which of our values we wish to live, and how we will contribute those values to society. In this way it is our free will, our freedom of choice as to what we create.

You could say, 'this is your group Startree, what do we want to grow on it?' Be sure they all have the opportunity of contributing. Mention you want their contributions because every child is important, and their words and values matter to this group. Some children will be more likely to speak than others, so ask every child to say a word from the Startree Creative Word list (see page 95) which is displayed on the whiteboard or a large sheet of paper. You can take the list from this book, and adapt or expand it appropriate to age. Ensure there are many words or you will limit their options, when the idea is to expand their options as much as possible. Mention the list is there as a guide, and that they can use their creativity to suggest values that are not on it.

When each child makes a suggestion, write their group list on a whiteboard or large piece of paper so everyone can see it. Some children may suggest the same value as another child, or one that is similar, but still add that word to the list. This way every child will see that what they say, and think, and value is important, even if ten other children have said it before them. The exercise has many levels, not the least of which is for each child to learn through experience that what they have to offer matters. Point out the possibly that a value of others may not be as significant to them. No value is more important than another; it is a matter of choice. We can all learn from this process, I know I have. Hearing the values of others and gaining insight into them can be a wonderful experience and opportunity.

THE LIST

The length of the list will depend on the number of children. We need ten values for the Startree illustrated in this book, so next put the values into ten groups. Putting the values into groups will set the scene for putting it into practice, which we do next. When grouping the list, one child for example may say 'love', another 'kindness', or 'caring', and these may be grouped together. Someone may say 'honesty', or 'truth', or 'sincerity', or 'genuineness', or 'integrity', and they could be grouped together. Explaining why they are so grouped gives you the opportunity of talking about values, their importance in our lives, and how they are enacted. With your explanation and creative contribution, the children will learn the meaning and significance of the value, and it will not remain merely a word. Keep it simple.

Ostensibly you are explaining why you have certain words grouped together for their Startree, while actually you have created the opportunity for teaching them the importance and consequences of values. By teaching this way you are giving the children a choice, and they do not get the impression you are telling them what they should do, for example, 'be honest'. Then have the children co-operate to decide which word they want from each of the ten groups, and put the ten values on the Tree. This is what the group wants to create in their classroom, their family, and their school. It is their Startree, and they have every reason to be proud of it, so display it somewhere prominently for all to see.

To give you some insights into interpreting the Startree, you might ask the children: 'Which word is written on the star at the base of the Startree, indicating the fundamental value on which you build your life?' 'Which word did you put on the star at the top, pointing to the value that overlights your life?' 'Which values were the core values along the trunk of the Startree, the solid, stable, strength from which all the other values branch out?' 'Which colours did you use for which words, and how do these relate to the information contained within the chapters on colours?' 'Did you start at the top or bottom of the Startree?' 'Did you start at the base, and work to the top, or at the top and work down?' 'Did you start in the middle, in the heart of the Startree?' 'Which values did you want as the mainstays of your life?' 'Which value did you choose to base your life upon?'

Remember it is important to recognise and let children know there is no right way to work with the Startree. You can change it at any time, and you can change it as many times as you choose. It is a testimony to your individuality, and you may find another value which you want to have grow in your life.

PUTTING IT INTO PRACTICE

The next step is to decide how the group or class will go about putting their Startree into practice. I do this by talking to children about a real tree and if we want fruit to grow, we have to take care of it, and nurture it, and be patient. I explain to them that like anything we create, it doesn't happen all at once, so 'don't try and do all the values on your Startree at once.' 'Just keep it simple and take it step by step.' The first step is for them to observe one value a week, and each child will have a turn at nominating the value. When they get to the end of the 10th week they will begin again. As the child nominates the value they can talk briefly about what this value means to them, and why they chose it. If, for instance, the value they select to create is 'friendship' invite them to suggest ways this can be enacted. While you were grouping the words, your explanation of the values and how they are enacted would have planted seeds for this. Maybe one way of showing friendship would be not to gossip, maybe it could be sharing, or being helpful, or forgiving, or understanding, and have them suggest ways they can do this.

Be sure there are plenty of suggestions, and make them feasible, not far-fetched, idealistic or out of reach. Keep it simple. Then the children decide how they will create that value during the week. Your group will be working together hand in hand creating a very powerful effect in your classroom, family, and school.
It is very important to explain to the children the value of learning by our mistakes, because they may feel ashamed if they do not carry out their values as they

had planned. Explain to them the benefit of making mistakes and cite an example of someone famous who tried to do something many times before succeeding. Talk about mistakes as practice. We may need to practice something many times before we can do it. Maybe this is an opportunity for you to mention the example of Michael Jordan the world famous basketball player, who I mentioned in the previous chapter. He is highly skilled at making successful shots with the basketball. You could ask them to think about how many times Michael Jordan would have had to throw the ball at baskets during practice before he became so skilled. The point being, if he thought he had failed because of all his missed shots, and given up basketball, he would not have become a world champion. He learned how to make the successful shots, because he used his 'mistakes' to see what did not work. By correcting his 'mistakes', he learned how to make the winning shots. So, in effect, he used his mistakes to learn how to achieve what he wanted. They can think about their mistakes as part of learning, and not see them as failures. They can see obstacles as gifts.

The reason it is essential to talk about making mistakes is that we do not want the Values Programme to become something children see themselves failing at. In creativity there are no failures. This programme is a way to talk to children about not trying to be perfect, and that they are enough as they are. Unless children have a sense of self and know they are enough, as adults they can believe that what they do will never be enough, what they think will never be enough, where they are will not be enough, what they are given will not be enough, and who they are with will not be enough. The stress and the spiral of these beliefs and subsequent behaviour can become intolerable.

ACTION PLAN

How can you make a difference in your life tomorrow, and the next day, and how can you give something to those around you? The difference you make will also make a difference to you. It can change your life. Make a decision to use the information in this book productively for the benefit of children, yourself, and others. Take action. Ask yourself, 'What do I want to do, and what can I do to make my contribution?' 'What do I have to give?' It is not about money, but that always helps. It can be a skill you have or information, something you know that you could share with another. Ask, 'What have I learned from the difficulties in my life that I can give to another?' Contribute in some way to charity or those less fortunate. No one else need know about it. It is the difference <u>you</u> wish to make.

If you have a dream, go for it. If you feel there is more of you to be expressed, go for it. Does this sound remarkable or too good to be true? It can be done, and you can do it. Remember that everything that has been created was first a thought in someone's mind. Use the power of your mind to create what you want in your life, and see it thrive and flourish. If you want love to grow, give love. If you want kindness in your life, give kindness. If you want friends, be friendly. If you believe there is a need, make amends and say you are sorry.

Find the Starchild within you and follow your star, the star of who you really are, and you will find this through the values on your Startree, the tree of your life. Our starlight is always there. Just because clouds cover it and you cannot see it, does not mean it isn't there. Our true light is the one we are meant to shine not the reflection of another. Everyone has the capacity to understand what it is they need for happiness and fulfillment. Apply your values where and when you can in your daily life. Today, whatever you can contribute to another, do it. Do it, however small and inconsequential you think it may be. It is an action of your values, and your values matter. You can make a difference when you have the intention to give to another human being, to give part of what you have and who you are. Take a value on your tree and see how you can live it for a day or a week. Give your value to people during the course of your day, and then choose another. Start where you are and take a step at a time. Do what you can with what is right in front of you. You don't have to go anywhere else, or be anyone else, be <u>who you are</u>.

Be grateful for what you have. Get a diary and write five things in it each day for which you are grateful. This will change your day and your life, because your focus will be on what you have, rather than what you don't have. What is special for you? Whatever it is, write it down in your 'gratitude journal' at the end of the day. It could be a sunny day, a rainy day, the smile of a child, the kindness of a friend, anything at all that has value to you. Have your child do the same. Demonstrating to a child the value of gratitude encourages the perception that no matter what is happening in our lives, we all have something to be grateful for. And we can miss out on the experience of gratitude, which is one of connection; connection to yourself, connection to others, connection to the world around us.

Do you take time to appreciate the colours and beauty of nature and the energy of a tree, for example? Perhaps you could illustrate to children your gratitude for the existence of nature and animals, the song of a bird, the mountains, rivers, oceans, dolphins, whales, cats and dogs, and the pleasure it gives you to look at these, even in a magazine. Children are more open to nature and life around them. Often by the time we are adults we think we are too busy for such things, consequently missing out on much that is there for us to enjoy, gifts of Creation, as we are. Encourage children to notice the different colours of the flowers, of the trees, of people. In this way they will be alive to the moment, and not busy with what has been, or what will be in the future, and missing the experience of what we all have to be grateful for now.

Your life has meaning because of your uniqueness, and the fact that you are the only person who can fulfill your contribution. Which values do you want to contribute in your life? Which stars do you want to shine? Remember you may not be able to choose your circumstances, but you can choose your attitude to your circumstances, using your inner freedom of choice to turn your life into an inner triumph. See your colours. Which colours are you attracted to? Do your colours say you need to be gentle with yourself, or give yourself the push you need to fly out of the nest? Have your children connect with their values through their

Startree. What do they want to shine in their lives? What do they want to shine into the world? Be more open to what is happening to you, to the present moment. Stay awake to the people and events that occur in your life.

See each individual as someone who has their Startree of life, their own colours. What can you learn from this, and how can you gain insight from the colours of another.

There is a way for your life to expand, and grow to suit your true colours. It is your right as a human being, and the right of every child.

STARTREE CASE STUDY

To indicate the way the Startree can be used to develop insights into children and their qualities and potential, I have included one Case Study of a child too young to write.

This Startree is that of Emi, a three-year-old girl, the daughter of the parents with a sushi bar. I used the pattern of her five-year-old brother, Kanji, in the previous chapter as a case study.

Throughout the day Kanji and Emi are confined to a space less than the size of a tatami mat, which is roughly the size of a bath towel, with no one to talk to, no books, and only one video. The little girl was given the tree to colour by Takako a student who attended my 3-day workshop on the information in this book.

Takako wanted to support Emi in a gentle way, so she used the Startree and information of colour gained in the workshop. Takako suggested that Emi could use crayons and colour the stars anyway she wished.

Emi chose violet and gold, and wanted to colour the remaining stars in blue. Blue, as will be explained in Chapter 14, holds the possibility of a distant mother or father, and in this case the child has two distant parents. Blue issues are about communication, and this little girl has no one to talk to all day and into the night, except her five-year-old brother Kanji who cannot cope with the confined space and stress of trying to be quiet and perfect, so he continually runs away.

When Kanji is gone, this leaves Emi on her own, and she is silent, and very lonely. Blue can be about loneliness, and the whole Startree is in blue, save Emi's own true colours sitting on the top, all alone. Emi possibly sees herself without any support below her. Blue can also indicate lack of nurturing from the mother, which is the case in this situation. Blue, the colour representing her parents is predominant in this Startree, showing how important they are, and how distant they are.

Gold can reveal how we value ourselves and the star at the top of the tree is gold, which could reveal Emi has an issue around self-value. Violet, here surrounded by blue, could suggest she has disappeared in relation to the parents. Her true colours, violet and gold, seem insignificant in proportion to the amount of blue. Violet can often suggest someone who disassociates, and does not want to be here, and as Emi often expresses how tired she is, it seems that she is struggling to know how to be present.

Takako said that Emi is lifeless, listless and both she and Kanji are despondent. Using the information gained from the workshop and insights about colours and how to talk to children while they are colouring their Startree, Takako was able to support Emi and give her a sense of her value. Emi needed to know she was like a star, and no one was the same as her, and to be talked to and given the nourishment and nurturing that she so desperately needed. According to Takako, Emi seemed to hang on to Takako's every word.

There are many ways to express individuality in colouring the Startree. No way is right. It is an individual choice, but it can tell us much about ourselves and others.

I have said several times how powerful our creative mind is. Below are two meditations using our creativity that also can be used to learn through colour choice more about ourselves and children.

Meditation for Children

'Make yourself really comfortable by sitting on a chair, or laying or sitting on the floor.

Gently close your eyes, don't squeeze them shut, just gently close them, and breathe out. Just notice your body breathing, especially the way your body breathes out. Let the chair or floor support you, and notice that your hands are not clenched, or tightly clasped. You don't have to make an effort, or do any work. You only need to breathe and your body knows how to do that.

Now using your creativity in your mind I want you to put yourself in a blue bubble, blue like the sky. And inside this bubble it is very safe, and very peaceful, and very calm, and very quiet.

Any thoughts that come into your mind, let them drift by like clouds in the sky, and then notice your body breathing again.

Using your creativity in your mind, and still with your eyes gently closed, I'd like you to think of your favourite place in nature where you would like to be right now. Maybe it is at the beach, maybe in a park, or a garden, or on a mountain: whatever is special for you. Some place where you would feel safe and calm and quiet. And at this favourite safe place, you can notice there is a special tree, which stands out. It is a very old tree that has one big star on it. It looks like a very friendly old tree. This tree is called the worry tree. What colour is the star on your worry tree?

That special star on the worry tree has a special job, and that is to take all your worries, so you don't have them any more. And what you can do now is think of something that worries you, and give that worry to the star on the friendly old worry tree. That special star on this friendly tree is there just to take all your worries.

Maybe you could think of another worry, and send that to the star on the friendly worry tree. If you have anything that is troubling you, anything at all, in even the smallest way, send it to the worry tree.

Have you got something else that is worrying you right now? Well, just send it to the worry tree. You can do this anytime you feel worried. When you notice that you are worrying about something, use the creativity in your mind, close your eyes, put yourself in your blue bubble, and go to the beautiful place where the friendly old worry tree is waiting to take all your troubles.

Perhaps at the end of each day, just before you go to sleep, you would like to visit the worry tree knowing that it is waiting to take all your cares and troubles from you. Just hand over your worries to the friendly star on the worry tree. Have you given all of your troubles to the worry tree right now? If you notice later that you have forgotten one, perhaps you could send it before you go to sleep tonight.

Soon it will be time to leave this beautiful place and come back to where you are now. Before you leave, remember that any time you need to feel calm and peaceful and safe, you can use your creativity in your mind, and put yourself in your blue bubble.

And knowing that you can go back to your beautiful peaceful place in nature any time you wish, I want you to slowly and gently open your eyes. Don't move quickly, just stay as quiet as you were in the beautiful place of nature, until you are used to being back where you are now. Take some long slow breaths, holding your breath in for the count of four, then breathing out. Then stretch your arms and fingers and legs and toes, and maybe stretch your jaw and neck, and wait just a few moments before you get up from the floor if that is where you chose to be before.'

Meditation for Adults

'Make yourself really comfortable either sitting on a chair, or sitting or lying down on the floor.

Just close your eyes gently, don't squeeze them shut, and allow the chair or floor to take all your weight. Notice your breathing, especially the breath out. There is no need to make any effort, your body knows how to breathe. You can just notice how that is.

Notice that your hands are not clenched tightly that they are loose and heavy. Any thoughts that come to your mind, just let them drift by like clouds in the sky. Do not struggle with them. Just let them go, and notice your breathing once more. Whenever thoughts come to your mind, notice them drifting by. There is no need to struggle or hang onto them.

Notice that you are in a blue bubble, and within this

blue bubble you are perfectly safe, peaceful and serene. This is a bubble of protection where you can go whenever you need a peaceful safe place. You can always have this bubble around you if you want.

You will notice that there is another bubble coming closer to you, and this is of a pale violet colour. Now send all of your worries, concerns, pain, suffering, sadness and anything you no longer need, over to the pale violet bubble. You may send thoughts, beliefs, old scripts, anything you no longer need in your life over to this bubble. And when you have completed this process, watch the pale violet bubble drift far away until it is out of sight.

You are safe and protected in your blue bubble. I want you to travel in another direction in the sky towards the stars, and as you get closer there is one star that is glowing more brightly for you. It is the star where you first came from. As you arrive, waiting to greet you, there are many beings who love you and know you well, and your return is a source of happiness and celebration to them. There is a sense of a happy reunion for everyone.

Running towards you with great joy is a group of small children, who are delighted to see and welcome you. You notice one child in particular, and this child looks very familiar, and you recognise it is you as a child. This small child has been waiting excitedly on this star for your return, and wants to be with you again. Perhaps you hold the child's hand, or maybe you pick the child up. Do whatever is right for your child and you. There is an exchange of great love and welcome and a sense of being together at last.

There is a deep warmth and completeness in this place and a sense of harmony and well being. You and your child go to a beautiful spot where you can be safely and happily together. No harm can befall you in this place, and it is safe to trust here.

Soon it is time to leave, so you take your small child and place it safely in your heart and together you are in your blue bubble ready for your return to earth.

Knowing that you can return to this star at any time, when you are ready, slowly open your eyes. Take some slow deep breaths .Gently stretch your fingers and toes, arms and legs, and maybe your jaw and neck. Take your time before you rise from the floor or chair.'

So far then I have tried to show how the use of colour can not only be an important way of expressing our own individual creativity, our inner map, but it is also a tool to help us identify and understand others and their inner map. The next chapters provide information to help you to know what each colour means and how you can use colour to find out more about you and others.

STARTREE CREATIVE WORDS

TRUTH
GRATITUDE
RESPECT
KINDNESS
GENTLENESS
LOVE
FORGIVENESS
TOLERANCE
AFFECTION
FUN
SELF-ACCEPTANCE
CARING
PATIENCE
CONSIDERATION
UNDERSTANDING
MUSIC
PEACE
SINCERETY
COMPASSION
TRUST
HOPE
HARMONY
GENEROSITY
FRIENDSHIP
COURAGE
CO-OPERATION

HUMOUR
HEALTH
CONTENTMENT
RECREATION
CURIOSITY
DIGNITY
HONESTY
FAIRNESS
LOYALTY
APPRECIATION
LAUGHTER
JOY
ACCEPTANCE
INTEGRITY
NURTURING
BEAUTY
CREATIVITY
SELF-RESPECT
HAPPINESS
STRENGTH
SPONTANEITY
COMMUNICATION
POWER
ENTHUSIASM
SELF-CONFIDENCE
PURPOSE

STARTREE

Colour Selection

#	Top	Bottom
	Royal Blue	Deep Magenta
1	Blue	Deep Magenta
2	Blue	Blue
3	Blue	Green
4	Yellow	Gold
5	Yellow	Red
6	Red	Red
7	Yellow	Green
8	Yellow	Blue
9	Turquoise	Green
10	Green	Green
11	Clear	Pink
12	Clear	Blue
13	Clear	Green
14	Clear	Gold
15	Clear	Violet
16	Violet	Violet
17	Green	Violet
18	Yellow	Violet
19	Red	Purple
20	Blue	Pink
21	Green	Pink
22	Yellow	Pink
23	Rose Pink	Pink
24	Violet	Turquoise
25	Purple	Magenta
26	Orange	Orange
27	Red	Green
28	Green	Red
29	Red	Blue

#	Colors
30	Blue / Red
31	Green / Gold
32	Royal Blue / Gold
33	Royal Blue / Turquoise
34	Pink / Turquoise
35	Pink / Violet
36	Violet / Pink
37	Violet / Blue
38	Violet / Green
39	Violet / Gold
40	Red / Gold
41	Gold / Gold
42	Yellow / Yellow
43	Turquoise / Turquoise
44	Lilac / Pale Blue
45	Turquoise / Magenta
46	Green / Magenta
47	Royal Blue / Lemon
48	Violet / Clear
49	Turquoise / Violet
50	Pale Blue / Pale Blue
51	Pale Yellow / Pale Yellow
52	Pale Pink / Pale Pink
53	Pale Green / Pale Green
54	Clear / Clear
55	Clear / Red
56	Pale Violet / Pale Violet
57	Pale Pink / Pale Blue
58	Pale Blue / Pale Pink
59	Pale Yellow / Pale Pink
60	Blue / Clear
61	Pale Pink / Pale Yellow
62	Pale Turquoise / Pale Turquoise
63	Emerald Green / Pale Green
64	Emerald Green / Clear
65	Violet / Red

#	Colors
66	Pale Violet / Pale Pink
67	Magenta / Magenta
68	Blue / Violet
69	Magenta / Clear
70	Yellow / Clear
71	Pink / Clear
72	Blue / Orange
73	Gold / Clear
74	Pale Yellow / Pale Green
75	Magenta / Turquoise
76	Pink / Gold
77	Clear / Magenta
78	Violet / Deep Magenta
79	Orange / Violet
80	Red / Pink
81	Pink / Pink
82	Green / Orange
83	Turquoise / Gold
84	Pink / Red
85	Turquoise / Clear
86	Clear / Turquoise
87	Coral / Coral
88	Green / Blue
89	Red / Deep Magenta
90	Gold / Deep Magenta
91	Olive Green / Olive Green
92	Coral / Olive Green
93	Coral / Turquoise
94	Pale Blue / Pale Yellow
95	Magenta / Gold
96	Royal Blue / Royal Blue
97	Gold / Royal Blue
98	Lilac / Pale Coral
99	Pale Olive / Pink
100	Clear / Deep Magenta
	Other Combination

Case Study 1

Case Study 2

Case Study 3

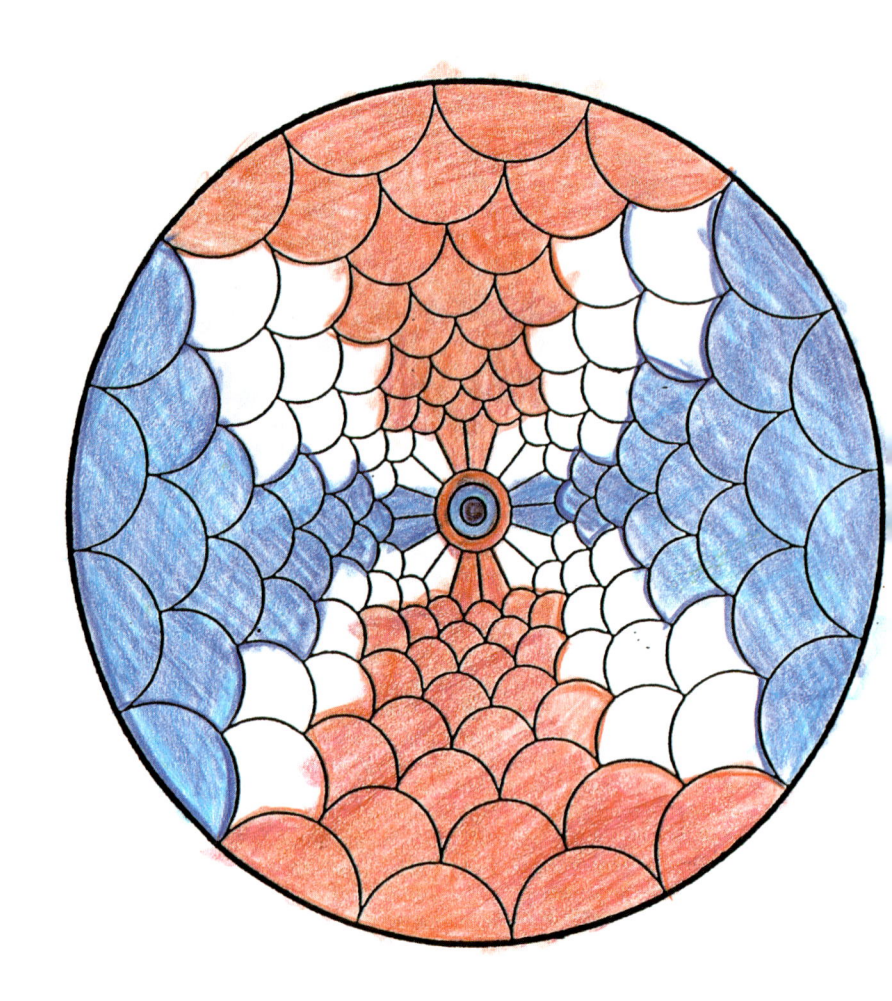

Case Study 4

Case Study 5

CHAPTER 5
YOUR TRUE COLOURS

Each individual child has the need to self-actualize, to be faithful to a genuine sense of self, its essential core. This process can be blocked, by the individual or by others, but nevertheless, each child has the need for authenticity and to grow in accordance with its intrinsic truth. Children are a gift. You are a gift, and worth the time it will take you. You are worth any effort it will take you, and the children are worth it.

In a world where 'big is better', 'more is better', 'degrees are better', 'get it right', 'be right', 'keep up', 'get ahead', 'achieve', there seems little room for the expression of acceptance and compassion for children as individuals. Each child is finding its way by expressing their different perspective, their own colour, and each is part of a united whole, the whole rainbow. Without being shown compassion, empathy and tolerance, a child cannot learn to be accepting of itself and others, accepting itself as it is with limitations and gifts together as one. Listen to the child within yourself and others. Seek the essence, the magic of the child, and the child within, the divine spark, the aspect of ourselves that is linked to the knowledge of why we are here: our true colours.

The intention and benefit of this book is building better relationships with each other, with children. It is about teaching by example, by showing children how to love, cherish and respect themselves, and giving them hope. Listening to children can give them a sense that they matter. Children are not born believing they do not belong. If this comes to them then it is something they have learnt, usually from adults.

A child needs acceptance, reassurance, patience, nurturing, protection, containment, touch, safety, unconditional love, acknowledgment, discipline, attention and respect. A child needs consistency so trust can develop. It needs to be reminded of its positive qualities more than the negative. It needs to be affirmed and upheld. This book is about upholding the worth of each person, and to validate his or her value as an individual. It is about saying it's important that you are here.

Do you feel you need acceptance, respect, tenderness, nurturing, tolerance, more happiness, or more kindness? When we feel safe, we feel we can try anything, we feel that we can do anything. Do you need to be acknowledged or validated? Do you need to be seen as you are? Would you like to be acknowledged? Are you afraid of making mistakes? Do you feel embarrassed if you have a feeling such as anger, pain, fear, grief, love, joy, sadness, self-pride, or the need for love? Are you frustrated with situations around you? Do you need more space in your relationships?

Do you feel alone? Do you feel that if you talked no one would really hear you? Do you have the need to talk, to be heard, and to feel connected to someone or something? Do you feel you have more to contribute?

Do you know what that is? Do you want your life to remain the same as it is now? Do you believe there are paths untrodden? Are you looking for something, and not sure what it is? Colour can provide insights and suggest answers to these questions as the following chapters show.

The world is different now to what it was fifty years ago. How do we live in this world in this new millenium? How do children? How will they combine the values and traditions of history and not make the same mistakes? How will they integrate these values with how different life is for them now? They know how. Trust them. They have their values, and they know what these are. They have their colours already, they were born with them, and they need their true colours to be nurtured, encouraged, protected, heard, and lovingly accepted. They need to learn that they have the right to be the way they were created. That is their birthright. It is the right of every child. All children are valuable. One is not better than another. One adult is not better than another. All are valuable.

There is such a short time for childhood, the time when a child can be cared for, nurtured, loved, have its needs met, have fun and play. A child cannot be expected to fulfil the needs of adults, or be expected to behave like a grown up, or to achieve beyond their capability or beyond their authenticity. Some children are good with their hands, and not with their intellect. Some are good with their intellect and not artistic. Not every one of us is an intellectual giant, not all of us are cover-girls, sporting heroes or medal winners, but we all are special in our own way. In our own way we have our gifts to contribute to our family, friends, our workplace, and to the world around us. There is a reason we're different. We are meant to be different. We all like different things. We all like to do different things, have our own thoughts, our feelings, and these are what make us unique. We have our own values, our way of viewing the world, our lens through which we see life, our true colors. These differences can come together to form a greater whole, a synthesis of colour, a rainbow.

The chapters that follow provide information about each colour. You will notice there are case studies included, illustrating how the colours operate in our lives. The case studies indicate a variety of trends. There are various possibilities held within each colour to give you insights, but please do not presume that every child will have every one of these issues. You will find some issues that appear in the colour relate to that individual and some not so much. Because of the uniqueness of each child, they will not essentially relate to every quality and characteristic held within their colour, so get a sense of which aspects apply to the individual. If the colour is the same in the top and bottom sections of the colour combination chosen, it indicates that the child has more of the issues. Remember that the bottom section reveals the more hidden aspects, and the top section that which is more obvious.

Feelings are a natural and valid part of the human experience to have and to use. There is information of the different feelings indicated within the colour information. The colours we have chosen reveal the feelings we are working with. Give yourself the gift of your feelings. Check your colours to see the possibilities you have to work with, and expand on these. Acknowledge the gifts you possess and the light you shine through the filter of your true colours. Reveal and release more of the fullness of your being. You are meant to shine, you are a star. So shine, light up the world around you with your uniqueness, and express your values and what you consider is important in the world. Give yourself permission to shine as the star you really are. You are created the way you are for a reason, and you have chosen the colours you want for a reason. Read about the colours you have chosen and see what they have to tell you, what you can learn, your gifts and possibilities.

You can make the difference to yourself and to a child. You <u>can</u> make a difference. You are <u>here</u> to make a difference. And the difference you can make does not have to be by inventing penicillin, or doing something world shaking, or something that will make the TV news, or the headlines. It can be in the simplest ways. Because after all life is more like that. Waking up, doing something meaningful with our day, meaningful to us. And what is meaningful will be found in your values and colours. It is about what feels right inside, not what others consider is meaningful. You do know deep inside, inside your heart, inside your being.

Use your colour selection to gain a deeper understanding of what is underneath the decisions you make. Learn to recognise your qualities and uniqueness. Each one of us has a child within who is trusting, loving, innocent, honest, precious, spontaneous, lovable, playful, curious, open, direct, creative, flexible, and has feelings. These qualities are integrated into the adult, so bringing to the individual the possibilities of a rich and fulfilling life, maximising its potential.

From your colours gather ideas and suggestions for handling situations around you. Awaken your true voice, it is never too late. To share one's truth allows others to know they are not alone in their confusion, fear, or pain. By sharing our humanness others recognise there are individuals experiencing similar thoughts, feelings, problems, and joys. Remember there is a meaning and a purpose to your life, so use the keys of colour to replace self-doubt. Believe in yourself. Go for it! Change can be challenging, scary, fun, healing, exhilarating, confusing, exciting, but never boring. Use effective listening to improve relationships with children, partners, family, business associates, friends, or clients.

Children need to know that they matter, and what they think matters, that their values and what they consider important matters: that what they do matters, and what they have to give matters. If the parent is not interested in a child this gives the child the impression that it is less important than whatever the parent is interested in, for example, work. Take time to be interested in what your child expresses, to hear their needs, and appreciate that they can have values that are different to yours, because no two individuals are identical. Children need to develop self-esteem inside, rather than believing it comes from outside themselves. If the child does not have the perception of self esteem, they will grow into adults who are prey to advertisers who tell them that a certain product will make them look better, more charming, sexier, appear smarter, look more successful, attract the right partner, have a better life.

Let your values and colours guide you. Use the information from your colour selection to gain insights, and enhance your life.

Here are some guidelines for the chapters on colours which follow. First, there are key issues, characteristics and possibilities held within each colour. In addition, for each colour there are potential opposite characteristics and possibilities. When I say, for example 'red people', I mean the colour red is in their blueprint. People 'working with red' are those who are dealing with issues related to red, or another specified colour, over a period of time.

Second, there are three primary colours, blue, yellow and red and all other colours are a combination of these three primaries in various proportions. The primaries are hidden within all colours.

Third, naturally enough, because most colours contain other colours, the messages of one may be embraced by another. A case in point is magenta which contains violet, so magenta may display aspects of violet within its qualities.

Where there are two variations of a colour there will be an overlap, for instance with blue and royal blue, and emerald green and olive green. Both blue and royal blue have communication issues, but each has a particular theme. Key issues of green are those of the heart, truth, and decisions. These issues relate to both emerald and olive green, but with an individual focus. While there are natural similarities between shades of a colour, each has a uniqueness of its own which will relate to the individual selecting it.

Where your combination contains the colour purple, read the chapter on violet; where it mentions rose pink, read the chapter on pink.

Finally, where your colour combination contains a pale colour, such as pale blue, or pale green, it means that the colour clear has been added. This will have intensified the issues of the colour it is with. Thus, pale blue is intensified blue issues, and pale green is intensified green issues. To gain insights into the colour 'clear', I suggest you read the information in Chapter 19. Where you have clear combined with another colour, you will need to read the chapters on both. If you have selected lilac, refer to it as pale violet; and lemon as pale yellow.

Coral can be seen as orange with the addition of clear, so not only does it have the characteristics unique to coral, there can be similarities with orange. In the case of pink it is a combination of red and clear, so firstly it has the characteristics and issues of pink, then there is the additional possibility of hidden intense red issues.

Rather than making it too complicated for yourself, I suggest you simply read your colours and those of your child, and look for hidden aspects later.

I have included affirmations which refer to the specific colours, and you can say these to yourself through the day if you so choose. There is a possibility that when reading such a book you may read the chapters on colours relevant to you or your children, friends, or relations only, and not read from cover to cover. With this in mind I have repeated certain key issues in various chapters throughout this book.

CHAPTER 5
RED

Red is hidden in pink, coral, orange, gold, royal blue, violet, magenta, deep magenta and clear.

Red is about energy and how we use it. It's about drive, passion and action, or the need for these. People working with red can be dynamos, busy doing many things at once and always on the go. They can be active people, who feel frustrated by inaction and the inability to move. Red people can really get things done, or seem to move mountains. Often they can feel burnout because they have used all their energy, and are depleted.

Red holds possibilities for determination, perseverance, initiative, indifference, domination, exhaustion, stubbornness, motivation, procrastination, resentment, passion, destruction, practicality, inertia, or endurance.

Red shows how we can react to life in the old pattern, or respond with new choices so creating the life we choose. Red is a dynamic and powerful color. Red asks, 'how will we use our power?' It can be power over, or power with; the power to create or destroy; the power to enrich and nourish, or deplete and drain. Red can build great things from small beginnings.

Red asks us to be awake to how we use the energy of our will, the will to live. For example, 'Am I being willful, obstinate and unyielding, or using my will for the greater good?' 'Am I using my energy to build or demolish?' Red can tend to outbursts of anger or frustration or violence. If children live with violence, they learn to believe that violence is the only way to solve problems. The undeveloped red will survive at all costs, and use their power and will to dominate or eliminate others. The other side of red will use their vigour and might, their strength and fixity of purpose, to build for the greater good.

Red shows the possibility of an adventurous, ardent, lively individual, who often goes where others fear to tread. If children choose red, provide them with plenty of activities and interests.

Children selecting red have expressed frustration at seeing what their parents and others do with their lives, and it is not what they want to contribute to society, or how they want to their world to be in the future. Teenagers know it. They don't know how to strike a balance between what they don't want and what they prefer, so they rebel, or feel hopeless, or act in destructive ways to others and themselves by, for example, doing drugs. There is a way to combine the old with the new and it is through the Values Programme, their Startree of life. Children do not want to demolish the world, they want to rebuild and expand the world, and they can often believe there is no way for them to do this. Where does this leave them? Where does this leave adults who have similar thoughts? The answer is in your values, and living them each day, step by step, showing your true colours in as many ways possible. There is a way for red to use its energy, drive, passion, and power in productive ways. Build and expand the world around you, and make a difference, with your value system.   Red can help gather strength inside for what I can, and am able to do. I can do it, and I will.

Red holds possibilities of guilt and shame. Healthy shame is when you make a mistake, and it can feel like embarrassment. Unhealthy shame is when you believe you are wrong in some way and can feel like 'I'm not good enough,' or 'I'm not smart enough,' 'I am not worthy,' or 'not deserving.'   People can have shame about their body: 'I'm too tall', 'I'm too short', 'too fat', 'too thin', 'too ugly'. Some people feel shame for existing if they were not wanted, and welcomed to the world when they were children. They express their beliefs that there is something wrong with them. They can believe they don't fit in, no matter how hard they try: that they are not good enough, no matter how much they try. They can find that success and love elude them, and can only be found by pleasing somebody else.

Because red is hidden in so many colours (e.g. orange, gold, coral, pink, royal blue, violet, magenta and deep magenta) these hold possibilities for issues of hidden shame. There is the possibility of hidden shame about our intelligence, intellect, or mental ability in gold. Let me explain how children can be shamed; it can be a situation where they were ridiculed, mocked, made a figure of fun, or made wrong, over some behaviour - something they did, or did not do. An incident where what they did or said was diminished. It can look like this, for example, say at school the child expressed an opinion and this was ridiculed by their teacher in front of other children. This can lead to a child who will not share what they think, or if they do express their ideas, they will feel embarrassed. There is the possibility of hidden shame about the way that we think, and embarrassment at expressing our thoughts in the colour Royal Blue.

Children, particularly boys, can be humiliated or ridiculed when they cried, if crying was not permitted in their family or school, and they believe there is something wrong with them when they cry in front of others. So from this experience children learnt to believe it is wrong, and consequently they are wrong, when they feel or wish to express an emotion. Girls feel shame and embarrassment when they cry in front of others, and try to hide or cover their face, or cover their eyes, so no one will see them in their embarrassment. Feelings and crying are perfectly normal human behaviours. If we were not meant to have feelings, we would not have been created with them. All feelings have a gift, and the gift of pain is healing, growth and moving on. The gift of shame is recognising our fallibility and humanness, and in this our connection with one another. We are all human, and need permission to have the feelings we were given as human beings.

Remember how much information about life is absorbed by children, without it actually being expressed. 80% of all communication is not verbal. So it can be that we were cut off emotionally by our caregivers when we were young, if we behaved in a certain way, and we quickly learn not to do that again. Maybe a parent or teacher was not pleased with our report card and would not speak to us, or if they did it was a sarcastic comment about our intelligence. We can be shamed or humiliated as children for having feelings of vulnerability, feelings of fear, feelings of anger, for thinking differently, for what we say, or for our need to be loved and nurtured. When these needs and feelings surface in our lives we feel shame, and blush, and don't want to be seen. Children can be shamed when they are unable to carry out a task that perhaps was beyond them, and they were expected to be bigger and more capable than they were. Children are not their behaviour. Behaviour is learned, and as they learn more, they learn to behave in a different way.

Some learnt scripts say that anger is wrong behaviour. However, in fact, anger is a feeling, not a behaviour. A feeling, and a behaviour are quite different. We are created with feelings for a reason, and every feeling has a gift. Anger is the energy for change. If we have been wronged or offended, healthy anger restores our dignity. What is important, is how we use the energy of anger. It can be enough to acknowledge to ourselves that we feel angry at something we perceive as offensive to us. Or we may use this energy to bring about a change. For example, the energy of righteous anger aroused in many people at the devastation caused by nuclear bombs and war, effected a change in attitude. Or some people feel righteous anger at the plight of the starving people in the world and want to do something about it. They use this energy for good.

Red is the energy for change or resistance. We can have resistance to feelings of vulnerability. When learning anything new, maybe a new behaviour, or changes in a belief previously held, resistance can occur and we revert to what we know is not the best way for us. When we are uncertain, resistance is a perfectly normal reaction. 'Will I let this information in, or will I push it away?' 'Am I ready to make a move towards changing right now?' Resistance can sound like, 'this is the way I have done it, and it might be uncomfortable, but at least I know it, and so this is the way I will do it'.

Each person has the right to be where he or she is in the process of his or her life. Red says 'do not shame yourself for being where, and how you are': 'Do not shame yourself if you are acting wilful and stubborn'. The other side of stubbornness is determination. You will move when you are ready. You will move when you are willing. Respond by detaching and allowing yourself to be where you are. It's human nature to hang on to what we know. Do not shame children when they are stubborn, they could be finding their own way.

Red suggests that you are patient with yourself in whatever is happening to you in your life. Understand that life is a journey, like a dance with movement and flow, and allow yourself to go with the flow and see where it is taking you.

AFFIRMATIONS
I AM NOW IN MY POWER

I AM NOW DETERMINED

I AM OK AS I AM RIGHT NOW

CASE STUDY 1

Tina brought her 9-year-old daughter, Sally, who chose red/violet. The child was subdued, and yet her mother said Sally was arguing with her older sister Michaela, was arguing at school, was not doing well in her grades, and was not 'the girl she used to be'.

Sally's father, Jack had left the family home and moved to another city, where he was living happily with another woman. Tina was quietly spoken, and resigned to the fact that she now lived with her two daughters and her mother Bridget. Sally had always been well behaved before and Tina was unsure what to do. She wanted me to 'fix' Sally so she would be 'the girl she used to be', and not cause Tina any problems.

Speaking to Sally, I discovered she was angry with her father for leaving them and taking away the life they once knew. She did not see her father, and possibly would not again. Sally was struggling with a new life, and a deep sense of loss for the way life was both at home and socially, as revealed in the violet. She had not cried, and instead of having her grief and loss, Sally used the energy in anger.

She felt shame at school because the family had broken up, and because she believed her father thought she was not good enough, and that is why he left. Sally believed she had failed somehow, and was not going to try again. Life with her father had been better, because he took care of everything, and her mother did very little. Sally also felt resentment towards her mother who now expected the girl's grandmother, Bridget, to take care of everything, including Sally, whilst Bridget had no patience with Sally or Michaela.

We talked about her anger, and Sally realised that she was not 'wrong', nor to blame for her father leaving. I explained that it is perfectly normal to have feelings in response to situations in our lives, and what is important is what we do with our anger. I made it clear that anger is a feeling, and not a behaviour, and she could choose how to behave.

Because Sally's previous life had disappeared, she was uncertain how to live without her father. It was difficult in the home of her grandmother with her mother Tina, who was grieving as well. The home was unhappy, and we talked about Sally's sadness, giving her the opportunity to release the pain she felt inside.

We spoke about how Sally could use her energy productively, instead of destructively, and we talked about her being a Starchild and she was perfect the way she was. When Sally did her Startree, she got the sense that she could do something to use creative words in her mind, and talk to herself inside her head in a different way.

Many children believe that the separation and divorce of their parents is their fault. And that the father or mother would have stayed with them if they had been better, or good, or more lovable. With so many marriages ending in divorce, this is a crucial issue for children. They need to know they are not to blame, and that who they are and what they have done, has not created this unhappy situation.

Sally needed to know that she was not responsible for the marriage break-up, and there was nothing she could do to change this situation. It was a relief for Sally to have this weight taken off her small shoulders. There was no one there to care for Sally, and give her the attention she needed in the home of her grandmother. Bridget ignored her because she was displeased to have the family living there, her mother was grieving and unhappy and wanted Sally to care for herself, and Michaela was feeling lost and had withdrawn. With all the changes, Sally misbehaved to get the attention she needed.

Sally could see for herself how much better she felt when she had some positive attention paid to her. She chose to work with the affirmation "I am good enough and okay as I am right now".

CASE STUDY 2

Mary, a 37-year-old woman with 3 children, was a part time office worker. She chose red/gold. She felt she had not done enough with her life, and that there was never enough energy to do all that was needed. She expressed being tired, frustrated with her life and there had to be something better than the existence she had.

The red she selected indicated a lack of energy and she said when she was younger she had so much more of a sense of aliveness, and energy spilling over. Mary wondered what had happened to her.

When we spoke she realised how much she had undervalued her intelligence, and worth (the gold issues), and lacked self-esteem. Mary had been convinced from her days as a child in the family, that only boys should gain an education, and that her life would consist of only looking after children, and doing unfulfilling office work. Mary earned a perfect score in Physics while a student and her father told her it was wasted because she was a girl. Because red is in gold, there was the possibility of some hidden shame or frustration around her intelligence.

As we were talking, Mary remembered her father saying that her grades were never enough, when in fact she was getting high marks. Her father was not happy that her grades were higher than those her brother received, and Mary had learned to undervalue her intelligence and resent her brother.

When she realised how valuable she really was, and that she could acknowledge herself, her intelligence, and her possibilities in life, Mary came alive. Her enthusiasm lifted, and she had a more positive approach.

She had always wanted to be a pharmacist and decided to study to fulfill her ambition by enrolling at University. Mary chose to work with the affirmation "I am intelligent and in my power".

CHAPTER 6
PINK

Pink contains hidden red and clear.

Pink is about being loved unconditionally. Often children were shown conditional love, which says 'I will only love you if you behave this way'. 'You will need to change or adapt if you want me to love you, because I won't love you the way you are'. So, as children our learned script says that in order to be loved we have to do something, or behave in a certain way, or look a certain way, or be a certain sex, or have certain grades. Children hear messages, sometimes from their mother, with expectations like: 'my son or daughter the doctor'; 'my son or daughter the lawyer'; 'my daughter the beautiful model'; 'my husband the achiever'; 'my mother the good cook'; 'my child the graduate'; and we see our purpose in being something for someone else.

This living for someone else sets us up as children to spend our lives looking for unconditional love and someone who will hear what is inside us and love us as we are. We can look for love outside, but it is <u>inside</u> all the time. Pink suggests we are created with unconditional, unswerving love. We are love. This is who we are. We are lovable. When we learn that we are lovable as we are with all our imperfections, we no longer need to hide them from others or ourselves, and try to be something else in order to be loved and accepted.

Pink offers the opportunity for forgiveness. Choosing pink, there is a likelihood you need to forgive yourself or others. Pink suggests that as a child, parent or friend, you could not do what you did not know. What happened in the past, is past. So forgive yourself. It is over. And the same is true for others, so forgive the fact that you did not have all that was needed in your life before this moment. The past is gone, and you can release yourself from it, by the act of forgiveness. When we don't forgive, we are the ones held in bondage. Forgiveness is an act of self-love, of self-caring.

Pink offers the opportunity of making other choices on how to care for yourself and others. Your choices will be indicated in your value system.

Pink is about caring, kindness, gentleness and warmth. Undeveloped pink may reveal subtle domination. Pink holds a likelihood of 'tough love', and the need to say, 'No'.

Pink understands there is a difference between someone saying they are listening to you, and you actually experiencing being heard. Your needs, thoughts, and feelings being heard. Pink children have the sensitivity and ability to hear and sense the needs of others, and very often experience intense frustration, when they believe others do not hear them. Because pink is about love, this can lead to feeling unheard and unloved.

If no one cared to listen to us as a child, we did not learn to listen to ourselves, and care for our own needs and feelings. This sets up situations of sacrifice in the name of love. Pink offers the opportunity of balancing love and caring for ourselves, with caring for another. Pink says 'I have the right to my need for care, and my needs are equally important as another's'. Pink affirms that you have the right to decide if and when you will care for others.

When we frequently sacrifice our rights, we teach other people to take advantage of us. In adulthood, not being heard as a child, can lead to choosing partners who also do not hear us. It can lead to relationships where we are expected to give love unconditionally, unswervingly, and consistently but we can believe that we are not genuinely being heard around our needs. We want the partner to hear us, but we have chosen someone who does not. They don't know how too. Pink suggests that when we learn to hear ourselves, eventually we will choose people who do the same for us. We won't settle for less. We don't want children to be in relationships where they feel unloved, or are loved conditionally. Pink knows the difference between selfish, self-less, and self care.

Pink suggests we are patient with ourselves while we learn to hear and love ourselves unconditionally, as learning can be a frustrating process. If you chose pink remember to be gentle with yourself and recall an example of a child learning to walk and the frustration it could experience at falling over. Remind yourself that this is the frustration of moving forward, not the frustration of going nowhere. It is the frustration of learning to walk, as opposed to the frustration of only being able to crawl.

Some learnt scripts say that in order to be feminine a girl should be passive, frivolous, powerless, dumb, selfless, submissive, domestic, obedient, and taking care of everyone's needs. Often she feels wrong as a female if she is not. Pink suggests femininity can include being intelligent, active, stable, and powerful. Pink affirms that a female may care for herself, and question what is happening in her life and her world.

Some scripts say a man is expected to know everything and have all the right answers. He is expected to be unemotional, be a good provider, be able to stoically endure without complaint, be invulnerable, be a hard worker, be rational, show no feelings, and have no needs. What if the man has emotions he wants to express? What if he does not want to work stoically without sometimes complaining? What if at times he is irrational, or feeling vulnerable, or does not have all the answers all the time? He can believe there is something wrong with him, or that he is not a man in some way. Pink says you are lovable just the way you are. Pink says you can be the man you choose. You have the right to be an individual. You have the right to be different.

As parents and individuals the best we can do for others in our lives, is to love and respect who we are, and be that. Be that. This in itself will pass on something, not only to our children, but also to our colleagues and friends, in our relationships at home and at work, as part of our expression in the world. It means showing caring, kindness and consideration to yourself, and becoming a role model others can learn from. You can become the powerful being you are.

Pink says I am lovable and therefore everyone else is lovable. When the world receives a child as they genuinely are, and they are welcomed and loved for being themselves, it can totally change the life of a child and its future. In turn this affects the future of those around it. The life of a child is worth this. Your life is worth this.

If you can give all that you are to the world, then the world will be a richer place because you were born. You were born the way you are for a reason. I don't know the reason, but in your heart you do. Find out what it is. Listen. Listen to the children. Listen to the child within yourself, and you will hear your own gifts, then contribute those gifts, and shine them into the world.

AFFIRMATIONS
I AM LOVABLE
I AM KIND AND CARING
I LOVE THE WAY I LOOK
I FORGIVE MYSELF

CASE STUDY 1

Sara, a girl who had just left school was struggling to know what to do with her life. She chose green/pink.

She was the third child, and knew from an early age that she was not wanted. Sara knew her mother resented her arrival when she said that Sara spoilt the life they had, and the family was happy until she arrived. Her mother told her it was a struggle to find the money for a third child, besides they had a boy and a girl, and did not want any more children.

From as early as she could remember, Sara knew there was no one there to hear her. She came to believe there was nothing she could do to get love from her mother. Sara expressed pink and green issues, when she said that she believed she gave out a lot of love, and yet her heart felt as though it had been broken. There were green issues regarding decisions that needed to made, regarding moving on with her life, which direction to take, and where to go from here. Yet Sara felt stuck, and unable to decide what was best for her. She had the distinct understanding that a positive new beginning was there somewhere, but where?

Sara had always compared herself to her brother and sister, and believed she came from a 'less-than' position. They each had a place in the family. Naomi was favoured by their mother, and Kevin by their father. Sara was envious of her siblings. At school she felt inferior, and it was as if she had closed her heart, and would not let anyone in. These are all green issues. Sara received no time and attention from her mother or father, and wished she had never been born. She felt extremely pessimistic.

We talked about the fact that she was born for a reason. That there was no other individual in the world who was quite like Sara, and could do what she could do. No one who could contribute quite what she had to offer. Sara had never heard anything like this before, and at first she wondered if this was the truth. She was indoctrinated with beliefs about her not deserving love, and being a nuisance.

Sara began to see that she had a place in the world, and was keen to discover what it was. Using the values on her Startree as a key to her heartfelt truth about what she wanted to do, Sara began to make decisions around which steps to take – these are green and pink issues.

Sara needed to know that her experiences were normal and human, and that there was nothing wrong with her. By reminding Sara that new beginnings and changes in our lives naturally bring a level of anxiety, it normalized her situation, so easing her concern. It was the first time she felt listened to, or thought she mattered because someone took her feelings seriously.

From then on it was one step at a time. The affirmations Sara selected were "I am lovable" and "There is space for me".

CASE STUDY 2

Beverley a 29-year-old woman had just been left by her lover, Seamus, and she was deeply distressed. She chose pink/violet. Seamus was a man she met through work, and he was married with a young daughter.

Beverley had a history of relationships with married

men who said they were unhappy in their marriages. She had no idea why this occurred. The men always left her after a short time and she was currently grieving yet again. This time she was desolate and believed she would never be truly loved.

As a child Beverley felt unloved after the birth of her brother when she was two years old. She remembered it quite clearly, and had never been given love by her parents from that time onwards. In fact they made it obvious to Beverley that she was second to her brother Paul, that she was to take good care of him, and virtually be at his beck and call. In fact, she became like a servant to Paul.

Beverley said she loved her brother, and yet deep down she was angry that he received love from her parents, and love from her, and yet love was not given to her by any of them. She had always felt unloved, and believed she had been searching for this elusive love all her life.

When we talked, Beverley had a great deal of unexpressed grief and pain regarding her childhood. She sobbed as she recalled how she was unheard around her needs, and that there was no one there to care for her. As a child she believed that somehow she was not perfect enough, or lovable enough and there was something wrong with her. No matter how much Beverley tried to please her parents by taking care of Paul's every need, they did not acknowledge her, and neither did he. Their parents taught Paul to expect this as his due.

Beverley came to realise that she was repeating the script she had learned as a child, with the men in her life. She chose men who were already receiving love from their wives, and then Beverley took care of their needs as well. She had never learned that her needs were equally as important as those of anyone else, so she always put herself second. Beverley had learned to sacrifice her rights, and so attracted others who would take advantage of her.

Beverley was a kind, caring and loving person, who wanted to be helpful to others. She needed to see that she deserved the same attention that she showed, and that she was perfect and lovable just as she was. These issues are part of the colours pink and violet.

Beverley liked the idea of writing "I am lovable" on small pieces of paper and placing them around her home. So whenever she opened the refrigerator there was a note reminding her she was lovable, when she opened her wardrobe to get dressed there was a note, and when she opened a cupboard for food there was another reminder that she was lovable.

She started writing a 'gratitude diary'; where at the end of each day she said thank you for five things. This brought her attention to all the ways she was receiving and enjoying love everyday. It changed her daily experience from loveless to loving.

Beverley chose the affirmations "I deserve love" and "I am lovable and perfect as I am".

CHAPTER 7
ORANGE

Orange contains yellow and red.

Orange is about connection with others. Orange is about enthusiasm, deep joy at being alive, or melancholy. Orange has vitality and shows an interest in life. It is about movement or being blocked. Orange is a regenerative 'get it together' colour. It can be full of promise, or may indicate that someone has forgotten how to live.

Orange children like to connect with friends as they can be very sociable, or they may have difficulty making contact with others. As a child there could have been some upset bringing a degree of shock or disconnection.

Orange offers the opportunity to break through when you are blocked or disconnected. Break out, break free, break the ties that bind you. Orange says 'let go and move on, there are many possibilities, so release past hurts, traumas or disappointments.'

Orange points to individuals who are tolerant, welcoming, and convivial; or perhaps controversial and discordant.

Co-dependence, independence, and interdependence are possibilities held within orange. Co-dependence says 'I cannot live without you'; independence says 'I can do it by myself'; interdependence says 'I can exist by myself, and you can exist by yourself, and we choose to be with each other: I am connected to myself as an individual, and I can connect with you.' These three issues are demonstrated to students in this simple way. I hold up one hand representing an individual, and hold up a second hand symbolising another individual. Then to illustrate independence, I hold my two hands at a reasonable distance from each other, symbolising strength alone. To represent co-dependence, I have my two hands grasping at one another. Then to illustrate interdependence, I bring my two hands together as they mutually support each other.

As human beings, we are meant to join together in a mutually supportive way. Orange suggests we need one another. If I am disengaged from myself because of some shock, disturbance, or upset, I could find it difficult to interconnect with anyone else. This results in an uncomfortable sense of division, dislocation or segregation.

A simple, yet highly descriptive overview of the qualities orange has as a colour, is illustrated by using the example of orange as a fruit. An orange appears seamless, yet consists of various segments, combined together to create the complete fruit. The individual pieces are separate and distinct, then attached and integrated to form something that is greater than each of the parts. An orange could be seen as fragmented pieces, or pieces which are self-contained. The segments seem identical, however when examined more closely, they are not precisely the same; still each piece is essential, as they blend and unite to form the whole. Oranges can be sweet or sour.

If you look closely at an orange, every segment is composed of many very small individual segments each quite separate and yet fitting seamlessly with the others. Each very small individual segment is significant in the structure of the orange, and similarly each very small individual segment is significant in the structure of the family, community, society, and country. Every individual is important. You are important. Every child is important.

Without the segments, there is no orange. A healthy orange only exists because of the health of every individual piece. So it is with society. In society, it is essential to respect the individuals, as they are the creators of society. Orange regards everyone as equal and universally connected.

Continuing to use the orange as an example, we can extend it much further. An orange is shaped like a circle, so is our planet earth. As each segment forms part of the orange, each country forms part of our planet. Every country shares the planet, and while each country is a collective complete with its own individual language, values and characteristics, each is interdependent on other countries to trade and share their gifts, in the form of natural or specialised resources. In this way each individual country is linked to others, and has something unique to offer, while remaining true to itself and its own values. Within each country, various areas have something to develop and contribute to their society as a whole. Within each area there are smaller communities, the contributions and resources of which are valuable. Then, within the family unit, your gifts and contributions are valuable. So too are the gifts and qualities of every child.

Orange may demonstrate purpose and productivity, or, alternatively, show someone who is holding back from life. Orange can be conciliatory, or on the other side, is contrary and contradictory.

Orange could reveal someone who becomes deeply upset, even traumatised, when they make a mistake, so they won't make a move at all. Orange may also have the tendency to try too hard.

Orange individuals can be courageous and undeterred, with a positive approach to co-creating in joint undertakings. The undeveloped orange person, however, could be disruptive, dissident and disagreeable. Orange says there is a difference between disagreeing, and being disagreeable.

Orange says you have the right to ask for help, to seek assistance, and to need another. The other side of this is a sense of deprivation and staying apart. Orange suggests we are individuals who have something to offer each other. I matter and you matter, and the union of our combined potential is a force greater than we are solo. We can come to relationships connected with our true authenticity and share this with others.

Orange supports you to have the fullness of your feelings, those aspects of yourself which form part of your unique chemistry. Connecting to our feelings is connecting to a source of rich possibilities. Orange reminds us that feelings are not behaviour. Feelings are a personal expression of our aliveness.

Orange encourages us to ensure our children connect to their aliveness, their authenticity, and their spontaneity. Authenticity means the special individual qualities, characteristics and gifts we were born with. The values with which we are deeply connected. Children know. They know their values and what they want in their classroom, in their lives, and in their world. Their Startree and their communication tell us this.

The child's pattern will indicate the individual approach to a given situation, and task. How does your child respond and connect? Is it different to you, to others? No way is right or wrong, it is just different. It gets to the same place, which is the completion of a task, however, the roads taken are vastly different, and consequently the journey is different. Orange suggests there is something to be learned from the way others perceive events and situations; how they connect with life. We can discover another piece of the picture, another viewpoint, another perception. We can learn from children.

Children need to feel they belong. Orange reminds us that a child's early attachments and relationships provide the basis for future relationships throughout their lives. If at this time they acquire a sense of identity and separateness, they will have a true sense of themselves and their rights, and so the rights of others. If their rights are observed, they will gain a sense of their intrinsic value, and that of others. Every child has rights as already indicated. These rights include the right to be loved, to safety, to be accepted, to kindness, to caring, to express their truth, to peace, and to their individuality.

Orange could be eager to please and acquiescent, sometimes losing themselves in the desire to become attached. Girls may believe they have to be a certain way to attract a husband because they have a message that to be married by a certain age is important. Then they will be seen as successful in the eyes of their friends who have also received this message. What if this does not happen? When they have a different experience to the messages they were given, the individual feels they have failed in some way. Boys may become stressed by striving to provide girls with a lifestyle they have been told is appropriate. To sustain this lifestyle they need to work in a job that is secure and gives them a reliable income, often without regard to the needs, gifts, or values of the individual.

We can be led to believe we have no choices, and that we are powerless. This is a reason why these days so many children and young adults are rebelling. These beliefs are not adding to their lives. They see the life their parents have led, and it does not fit with their values or the meaningful way they wish to contribute to society. Orange says connect with your values on the Startree. Which values do you want to shine in your life?

Orange suggests that you become more aware of what is happening to you in each moment, your feelings and thoughts. Connect to others and stay open to the people and events in your life. See each individual as someone who has their Startree of life, their own colours. What can you learn, and how can you gain insights?

Orange inquires 'do you take time to connect with the world around you and appreciate the colours and beauty of nature, for example, flowers and trees, the song of a bird, the mountains, waterfalls, rivers, ocean, dolphins, whales, cats, or dogs, and the pleasure it gives you to look at these, even in a magazine'. Often by the time we are adults we think we are too busy for such things, and so miss out on something that is there for us to enjoy, a part of Creation, as we are.

Orange says that by staying alive to the present, and not busying ourselves with what has been in the past, or what will be in the future, we experience what we all have to be grateful for in each moment.

Orange holds all in equal regard. Orange says society can be seen as an orchestra, and each individual is like an instrument having a part to play in the symphony of life.

AFFIRMATIONS
MY LIFE IS FULL OF PROMISE
I AM CONNECTED AND MOVING IN MY LIFE
I AM BREAKING THROUGH MY BARRIERS

CASE STUDY

Margaret, a girl in her teens was having difficulty leaving home, and going away to college to study. At the thought of being away from home she would panic, become very fearful, and she was having difficulty talking about it. Margaret chose blue/orange.

When we spoke she remembered her first day at kindergarten. She had been traumatised when her parents took her there because they did not tell her she was to stay for the day only. She believed they had left her there forever. When they left her in a strange place she was shocked and very frightened and did not speak to anyone all day; orange and blue possibilities. Little Margaret expressed huge relief when her parents returned in the afternoon, because she thought she would never see them again.

To go to school each day after that was a repeat of the terror, and it took Margaret some time to begin to trust. She remembered this event for many years, but thought that because she was a teenager now, the intense feelings would have diminished. Margaret believed that at her age she 'should know better', but still felt unsafe. These are issues which relate to the colour orange.

After she realised that an event in childhood can have an impact and lingering memory for years, Margaret could normalise her intense fear at leaving home now. We discussed the blue issues Margaret was dealing with as well. In her case, blue indicated a need to learn to nurture herself, communicate how she felt, and not to withdraw and try to work it all out in her head alone.

She began to have faith in herself, and slowly trust talking to others.

Because Margaret said she was constantly jumbled and nervous inside, meditation proved to be very useful, and she was able to find a peaceful place within, which she had never experienced before. She had literally never felt really safe after that childhood experience, when her parents had laughed at her for being so silly, and had not comforted or nurtured her, very much a blue issue. They said of course they were coming to pick her up after kindergarten, she should have known that. In truth, how could she know that, if they did not tell her?

The teenager had spent her life believing she should know information that she had not learned. Hence her expectation that she 'should know' what to do in her current situation. As a child Margaret said her parents were distant and did not communicate with her. Margaret was expected to know what to do without any guidance or nurturing, possibilities in blue. Her parents were totally disconnected from her, and from a young age she had to rely on herself. In effect she was expected to be an adult when she was only a child. There was no one to trust.

The difficulty was, how could she know what to do when she was a small child, so she believed she could not trust herself either. She would come home from school, go to the kitchen and ask questions of her mother, who would say, 'don't ask me, you should know'. This left Margaret believing that asking for support was wrong, so she tried to work things out in her head, which is impossible for a child. She would then experience deep nervousness, a sense of being separate and disconnected, and would not know what to do. These situations are relative to blue and orange.

By saying her affirmations to herself when she felt nervous and disconnected, she began to gain a sense of calm. She learned that during these moments, talking slowly and calmly to herself was what she needed, and then she would feel safe. This was a way of nurturing herself, and utilizing the qualities in blue. Margaret gradually learned to trust herself in situations where once before she would panic, become disconnected, and be unable to move.

She chose to work with these affirmations whenever they applied to her situation. Her affirmations were "I am safe", "My life is full of promise", and "I am connected and moving in my life".

CHAPTER 8
CORAL

Coral contains yellow and pink.

Coral is about sharing love and having it returned. Coral is amiable and has fun interacting within a group experience. Coral has a natural curiosity and spontaneity. This is particularly evident in children.

Coral can be community minded, concerned and sensitive to others, and demonstrates a social conscience. Coral is loyal and consistent.

There is often a sense of inclusion and bringing together with coral, or a sense of exclusion, exile or being lost.

Coral can be seen as orange with the addition of clear, so it has the possibility of intense orange issues. Potentially coral understands the value in harmonious co-existence, and sharing the qualities of all. Coral recognises the value of claiming your individuality, then being able to affiliate with other people to form a network for mutual benefit.

Coral perceives the richness of community association, and the contribution of teamwork. Coral works well in group situations, or could have difficulty integrating and believing they belong.

Coral enjoys a shared journey.

There is a likelihood of longing to be attached to someone or something. Coral may point to an absence or fear of love, or perhaps lost love. Maybe there has been an intense trauma at being shut out, being different and not being accepted or included.

Perhaps there could be challenges for coral individuals concerning intimacy and separateness. Coral reveals a tendency to cling to others, or the reverse, which is pushing people away and living like a hermit.

Coral sees that the collective possibility in society is greater than the single force. Coral knows how to intertwine various abilities into a co-operative, cohesive whole.

The undeveloped coral illustrates an individual who tends to only express the culture of the group. Perhaps the desire to belong leads them to conforming, and losing their identity. They may become passive, agree with everyone, and not have an opinion of their own.

Coral understands the richness of a social group united for the common good. Frequently they are environmentalists, concerned with ecology and the global viewpoint.

Coral shows team spirit, and is content with the inclusive mindset, recognising that each person has something to contribute for the advantage of all. The other side of this aspect, is an individual who is unable to assimilate and participate fully.

Coral offers the opportunity to be embraced and share your life.

There is the possibility of realizing the balance between giving and receiving in coral. Of being comfortable within the realm of independence and dependence, and the tension and movements between them. Or, perhaps there are unresolved issues in these areas.

Coral says, 'we can do this together: our combined power is stronger than one person alone. United we stand, divided we fall.' When we consolidate our individual strengths, we can achieve the optimum quality for the greatest number.

Coral is friendly and open-minded and enjoys the differences of others; or finds this challenging. Coral offers the possibility of updating our understanding of ourselves in relation to another. We don't have to know everything. Coral says 'learn by listening'.

With coral there can be a learnt script message that says, 'I won't grow up and then I'll be loved. If I stay helpless and small, maybe I'll be taken care of, and won't have to take responsibility for myself'. Coral may try to keep others dependent on them, in order to gain a sense of importance.

Coral shows finer feelings and concern for everyone else, whilst their needs are not always recognised by themselves or others. Coral suggests learning to love and accept yourself as you are, and allowing yourself to be different.

How can the ordeals you have endured add meaning to your life? Coral suggests considering the uses of adversity, assessing what you have gained, and sharing this as part of your contribution to society. Your life experiences are valuable.

Coral frequently demonstrates a moral vision.

AFFIRMATIONS
THE LOVE I GIVE IS FREELY RETURNED
PEOPLE LIKE ME, AND I LIKE PEOPLE
I BELONG

CASE STUDY

Lesley, a 31-year-old woman, who expressed a huge amount of frustration about her ex-lover, chose coral/turquoise. She had given love to a man, who told her he did not love her anymore, and that she was not to come back and make a nuisance of herself by visiting and telephoning him. He told her she was ugly. She expressed loving him so much she thought she would die when he said this, and did not return her love.

Lesley had felt unloved all her life, and believed she had met the love of her life when she met Lee, who is now in love with someone else.

Lesley believed that no one will love her or care for her, in the way this man did when he professed love for her in the beginning of their relationship. What she did during their affair was to constantly give Lee gifts, and pay for everything including outings and holidays. She was satisfied to do this, without him returning her favours. It was enough for her that Lee said he loved her.

Lesley was convinced her life was over now that he was ignoring her, and she constantly visited his home, and made many telephone calls begging him not to leave. She cried herself to sleep at night, and did not know where to turn. Lesley said she felt embarrassed at the way she kept going to Lee and begging, but she wanted things to be the way they were.

In her session, we spoke about the coral issues of learning to love yourself, listening to your own needs, and being gentle with yourself. Lesley had not realised that she deserved to be loved, and from childhood where she was the eldest child, she felt that she was supposed to take care of others. This is often the case with first born children who feel responsible for the others in the family.

Lesley began by accepting herself the way she was, and learning to listen to what she really needed. She was relieved to have the sense of forgiving herself because she felt intense shame, and underneath was angry with herself for begging Lee to come back. Lesley came to see that she had never in fact received love from Lee, and found that she was thankful that the relationship had ceased.

The break-up gave Lesley the opportunity to really see her pattern of giving love to those who would not, or could not return it, an aspect of coral. When in fact as she began to care for herself the way she had always cared for others in her life, she felt a warmth and security she had never experienced before.

Lesley was very hurt when told she was ugly, so each morning she would look in the mirror and tell herself how beautiful she was. At first it was strange for Lesley, nevertheless she persevered because she wanted to ease the hurt. The difference in her attitude to herself was noticeable after about one month, and Lesley became so much more self-accepting and comfortable with how she looked.

Lesley chose to say these affirmations whenever she had the need. "The love I send out is freely returned", "I am learning to love and accept myself" and "I am a beautiful person".

CHAPTER 9
GOLD

Gold contains yellow and red.

Gold is about the value we learn to put on ourselves, our self worth, and this begins in childhood. Gold can reveal the individual has some confusion about their value, and can believe they are only valuable because of what they achieve or what they possess. Gold says, 'know you are valuable as you are. Do not define yourself by what you have, or what you own, or what you do: or what you don't have, don't own, or don't do.'

Children learn to define themselves by exteriors, and forget who they really are inside. Gold individuals need to know they are always valuable and precious, no matter what they do or have. Gold values itself and others. Developed gold says, 'I am valuable, you are valuable, everyone has value.' Undeveloped gold says, 'I am more valuable than you.'

Gold can reveal a positive approach to life, a sense of excitement, aliveness, and joy.

Gold shows a sense of humour. Gold can be tolerant or, alternatively, narrow-minded. Gold suggests someone who may need to have more fun and joy in their life.

Perhaps someone who has self-doubts. Maybe gold judges itself or others. Judging says 'I am worth more or less than another person.' Gold indicates self respect, and respect of others. Gold knows how to reassure others, and reveals the possible need for reassurance.

Gold reveals the courage to feel the fear and do it anyway. On the other side it may suggest a tight control that says 'I have to know everything before I take a step.'

Gold shows an inquiring mind, possibly an intellectual. Gold can enjoy learning and studying, or really dislike learning and studying. Gold is intelligent, and often an inspiring teacher who makes learning a joy; a very wise individual, frequently at a young age. Gold can be playful. Do you need more time for play? Gold shows we are happy with who we are, or, not happy with who we are.

Gold says that whatever happens to a child, they think it's their fault. The details of the story are different, but the pain is the same, the loneliness the same, the sense of lack of self worth is the same.

Sometimes gold can have issues around money, in that people believe they don't deserve to have the good things in life. Somehow they are not worth it. The undeveloped gold believes money is everything. They can have all the material possessions, the things that should make them happy, but inside in their quiet moments they have no idea who they are, or their true value

The fear of being different, of not valuing themselves, the fear of being wrong prevents most children from learning to trust their inner wisdom, so they go along with the crowd. They learn to conform rather than question. But it is only when we look in the mirror that we see the truth of who we are.

Gold says joy is our birthright, but often children learn we are not supposed to be happy.

Gold can have a longing for something else. One of the biggest gifts we have been given is choice, which is the cornerstone of our lives. Gold says understand you have a choice. Gold affirms if you change your mind, you can change your life. Change how you view the past, and see it was a learning to get you here today. See the past, all of the past, as valuable.

AFFIRMATIONS
I AM VALUABLE
I DESERVE THE BEST
I HAVE THE RIGHT TO BE TREATED WITH RESPECT

CASE STUDY 1

Bob a 36 year old businessman, whose marriage had recently ended in divorce, was reassessing his life's direction. He chose green/gold. He had spent his life going very quickly, always in a hurry to make as much money as he could. Bob gained his value through work, and saw that making money and having prestige was his key to success in the world.

Bob believed wealth was worth, and yet he was finding these days that his wealth and success did not bring the security and happiness he thought it would. Deep down he had a belief that the success and money would somehow disappear, leaving him a failure without anything. Bob found his money and possessions did not ease his sense of insecurity, and his wealth did not bring him any comfort. His focus on work had cost him his marriage, and yet he said at that time he believed he was also working for the security of his wife, Peggy, and their two children.

He believed he was straightforward and honest with Peggy and their two daughters, and yet Peggy told him he was judgmental, and she could not live with his constant criticism of her and Katy and Susan. After his marriage breakup Bob was left wondering about his judgment issues, and could see he was very hard on himself, and on those around him. Peggy believed she was not a good enough wife and mother in Bob's eyes.

Bob was the second child and remembered always believing he was never as good as his older brother, Daniel. Whatever he did at school his parents always criticised and judged his efforts as not equal to the worthy efforts of Daniel, who they said was more intelligent. Bob wanted to please his parents, and believed he never did. He said he thought he was a failure as a child. He would come home from school happy with his work and good marks, and yet it was never enough to gain the praise and acknowledgement he needed as a child. He wanted to prove to his parents he was good enough, and thought they would give him respect, if he gained respect in the business world.

Bob saw he had a deep-seated inferiority complex and fear of failure, which he tried to hide by being seen as a success by others. He had never felt like a success inside, and in his mind he could still hear the judgment and criticism of his parents. When this became unbearable, he would find himself judging others. He realised he had been repeating his family pattern with his wife and daughters, and was unhappy that this had been the case. These issues are possibilities held within the colour gold.

Bob needed to see what he really valued in his life; not what he had been told was valuable. He already realised that when he accrued what he previously believed was valuable, it did not bring him any comfort or sense of worth. Bob came to see he was looking for his worth on the outside, and it was on the inside. He was trying to gain esteem from others, and this was proving an endless effort that brought no satisfaction. Bob needed to know he was enough as he was, and learn not to judge himself or others. These issues are also found within the gold possibilities.

When Bob became an adult, he believed that if he had money and prestige, he would never again feel the heartache and sense of worthlessness he experienced as a child. And yet, this was exactly how he felt again now. He felt broken hearted that his life had come to this, and wondered if it was too late to start anew, and find out who he really was, and what he really wanted.
The green in his colour combination indicated Bob was

at the point of making choices about the direction of his life, and he wanted to move and change, but felt stuck. He was uncertain what would bring him the balance and harmony he wanted.

He realised that he needed to take more time for relaxation, and not be in an endless rush trying to run away from himself and his inner insecurity. Bob also began to think deeply about his life's direction, and recognised that his focus had been on work, and he was not finding any enjoyment in life. He sought more of a balance between work and outside interests. Bob mentioned that he enjoyed music and found it very relaxing, so he thought he would like to have an interest totally outside his experience, to see if he enjoyed it, and he decided to learn to play the guitar. This proved really rejuvenating for him.

Because Bob needed to open his life, see what really had meaning for him, and understand what he considered truly valuable, we spent some time on his Startree and key values. Bob realised when he lost his family, just how valuable they were to him, and part of his new beginning was to spend more time with his daughters, being the father to Katy and Susan he had never been before. This area of his experience opened up and he could see that his focus at work was heightened when he was more relaxed, and there was more of a balance in his life. The quality of his productivity increased.

He wanted others to benefit from his new found learning, and decided to have meetings and talk to his staff about the need for balance in their lives, and to give them a sense of their true value and purpose in life.

Using the colour pattern and their responses, Bob found that he was able to place staff in the situations which suited them, which naturally, in turn, was to his company's benefit.

This had such a positive impact on staff morale, that he could see the importance not only to his company, but also to others. Bob is an astute businessman and was seeking a new direction and business ventures in line with his values, so we developed a values programme incorporating the positive feedback from his staff regarding what they learned by using the pattern and Startree.

In the values programme we included statistics about the increased staff work output, due to enhanced morale when they gained some balance in their lives, and sense of self worth. This programme has worked in various situations for other organisations, providing Bob with the understanding that he is contributing something worthwhile. Bob said it gave him a sense of fulfillment to see his life's experience was benefitting others, both personally and financially.

The affirmations Bob chose to work with are "I am enough and valuable as I am", and "There is balance in my life"

CASE STUDY 2

Margo is a 42-year-old woman who chose magenta/gold. She was having difficulty feeling safe in her life. Margo had a fear of expressing to others how she felt, and was insecure around men. She wanted to be with other people, yet felt nervous being who she really was in case they rejected her.

As we spoke, more details of Margo's life story emerged. Somehow Margo always expected the worst in situations which were occurring in her everyday life. She expressed being fearful when the doorbell rang, or when the telephone rang. She would wake up each morning afraid and apprehensive, and had experienced this underlying sense of fear through her whole life. Margo said she did not want to live the rest of her life this way, she wanted to have an easier life.

Margo remembered as a child always feeling fear at home. Her father Robert was an alcoholic and when he came home his moods would swing from elation to aggression, and all points in between. As a child Margo carried a sense of apprehension in her daily life because of the unpredictability of her father, as he would often vent his anger and frustration by beating her.

Anne, Margo's mother, was angry and fearful waiting for Robert to come home from his drinking bouts, not only because of his mood swings, but also because of his diminished pay packet. Robert's spending of money on alcohol created an ongoing economic struggle. Anne knew from long experience that he would be home with little money and she took this anger out on Margo because she could not get any satisfaction from Robert.

Margo felt shame because of her father's secret addiction and shame when he was hitting her, even though none of this was her fault or of her doing. She had low self-esteem and lacked confidence, as suggested by the colour gold. Anne tried to hide

Robert's drinking and put on a flawless image for family, friends and neighbours, and Margo was expected to be a faultless child. She believed that if she was super perfect, as her mother wanted, her mother or father would give her some love and attention: this is a magenta issue.

As a child Margo had a deep and intense loneliness, and because she was unloved, believed she was unlovable. She felt the need to express a deep wordless suffering contained inside her, and sobbed these feelings of loneliness, grief and pain so long unexpressed. Margo had been holding this deep within all her life, and she said the relief was enormous.

She said she had been afraid to start crying because she may not stop, and I encouraged her to have the feelings, as they would stop of their own accord. At the end of the session she said there were more tears deeper down, and that now she felt safer to have them. This can be an expression of the colour magenta.

Margo had been virtually abandoned as a child by being expected to be an adult and super perfect: these possibilities are held in magenta. She had no idea of her own value and lacked self-confidence, and did not perceive herself worth loving: issues held within gold. Her fear of the telephone or doorbell ringing was an echo of the fear held within her since childhood. Margo spoke about this early life and it was healing for her to be heard around how it had been, and experience compassion and acceptance.

Margo used the positive aspects of magenta to re-affirm herself each day and wrote out a series of affirmations about herself and her values from the Startree. She made a tape recording of these words with music that she enjoyed playing as background. Margo would play the tape to herself each day, or as many times a day as she believed necessary. Playing the tape and using affirmations was an act of love towards herself, and Margo experienced a deep calm whilst listening to the relaxing music and loving affirming words.

Because she was 42 Margo felt regret that so much of her life had passed without that deep love she needed. After listening to her story, and acknowledging the difficulties she had experienced, I asked Margo was there anything positive that she could see had come from her experiences, something that had meaning in her life. Margo said 'yes', she had learned not to be judgmental towards others, and to show compassion: again possibilities held within magenta and gold. Regardless of the fact that she lived in a loveless home, or perhaps because she did, Margo held firm to her belief in love and in loving others. Her beliefs in trust, love and compassion had become deep and abiding.

Margo found putting her values from the Startree into practice each day extremely empowering, and it provided a distraction from her fears as she slowly learned to trust other people. Margo could have a meaningful life while she was in the process of healing the past, and using her life and experiences for others. She encouraged people she knew to work with the Startree and incorporate their values into their lives.

Margo chose the affirmations "I am valuable and lovable", "My life has meaning" and "I deserve joy in my life".

CHAPTER 10
YELLOW

Yellow is also contained in orange, gold, olive green, emerald green, and turquoise.

Yellow is interested, spontaneous, and has a sense of fun. Yellow is curious and discerning, inquisitive and seeking. It may be quick witted and funny, or sarcastic with a sharp tongue. When they are worried, yellow individuals can go round and around in their thinking, and get themselves even more worried and uncertain. Yellow people can be assured or, alternatively, confused about themselves. Yellow people could have insecurities, and be afraid to look at them.

Yellow shows a sunny disposition. Yellow can be playful or timid. They are happy or apprehensive. Yellow could have a need for validation. Selecting yellow suggests the possibility of a need to eliminate something from their life, and there may be concern about dealing with this. Yellow asks, 'do you need to get rid of something?'

Yellow people can absorb facts quickly or, on the other hand, think they can't. They are usually intelligent, but could have an issue in this regard, and believe they are not. Yellow children may be academically inclined. Or the other side of yellow says 'I am not really intelligent, I cannot think', and these children become too nervous to ask for information that they require. In this way yellow can place over emphasis and importance on the value of academic qualifications. Academic achievement, diplomas and certificates are not a measure of the child's value; the child is already valuable. There is no measure that can be put on the value of children, and they need to learn that, intrinsically, they have value. The qualities a person has to give, the values they can bring to their endeavours, are more important than the piece of paper. People are our resource, and the uniqueness they bring to a situation. Yellow says, you are a valuable resource whether or not you have a certificate. A certificate is valuable, but not as valuable as you are.

Yellow suggests someone who likes to take control, and can be unwilling to let go of control. One way this can manifest, is for yellow to stay in their head so keeping away from feelings, which may be seen by yellow as messy. This would be experienced as 'I'll think and not feel'.

Yellow can indicate excitement, or, the other side of this, is tremulousness. An example of a yellow experience could be learning something new and then alternately feeling nervous, or excited. Mentally yellow can be experienced as, 'I am confused', or 'ah-hah, I understand'. It could be experienced as, 'I am excited because I am learning this' then, 'I feel fear because I can't grasp this'; 'I am mentally stimulated because I am learning this', or, 'I am confused when I am learning this'; 'something is about to happen in my life and I feel excited', or, 'something is about to happen in my life and I feel nervous'. So, the yellow experience can be up and down, up and down.

As children we need to learn that all our feelings are normal and, to understand this. We need to have our feelings validated, for example, fear. Fear is an emotion of degree, and on a scale it ranges from slight apprehension, to uncertainty, hesitation, shyness, nervousness, lack of confidence, awe, anxiety, or trepidation. The other end of the spectrum is, being scared, frightened, or alarmed. We need someone to hear our fear who listens, and doesn't tell us there is nothing to be afraid of. We need to learn that the fear will have a beginning, a middle, and an end.

Yellow says it is important to understand that the energy of fear is aliveness, it keeps us alert. It teaches us discrimination and discernment, and when to take care of ourselves. Fear and excitement are two sides of the same coin. Every step in life involving change has the possibility of a level of fear, for example apprehension or uncertainty, and this is a normal part of existence. If we are literally afraid to feel fear because it has negative implications for us, it becomes difficult to move, change or try something new. Yellow says to remember the other side of fear is excitement and aliveness, and then subsequently joy at the change. Fear, and the energy of it, is an essential ingredient in moving on.

Feeling fear in its many forms is an everyday experience. The common form of fear in yellow is stress. It can begin as a simple worry or concern. Concern that 'I won't be able to do this', or fear that 'I won't get this work done on time'; or 'will I get married?'; or maybe, 'am I being a good parent?'; 'will I pass this exam?'; 'will I get this job?'; 'will I keep this job?'; 'can I afford my expenses?'; 'will my family be okay?'; or, 'I am stressed because I have concern for my husband who is stressed....he has stress because of his concerns at work'....and so it goes on. A way through is to name the concern to someone you are safe with, and to be heard around the issue. The energy contained in the emotion is released and you are free to deal with what is happening. We can stand back, look at what is going on, and then act appropriately.

Children are stressed too. It is difficult if we have a belief and concern that we are not enough, or that we will not be enough for some person, situation or event in our lives. For instance, children express concern that they will not pass their exams and will be a failure if this happens. This and other concerns cause stress and anxiety in children, issues like, 'I am afraid I am not good enough', or 'I am too much trouble'.

This is why children drop out. They believe they are not enough, that they cannot cope with the pressure that is being put on them, that they do not matter as an individual, and that they cannot do it and will fail anyway. So they turn their attention to something they can do, anything to get away from the stress that they are not enough, or they will be rejected if they get it wrong, or that what they do will never reach the impossible standards which are placed upon them. There can be family or scholastic expectations placed on children, a perception that to be this or that in society is successful and will be an achievement, and if you do not attain these, then you are a failure.

Children are taught to chase the symbols of success to give them value, and not taught to value themselves.

Children and adults can struggle. They struggle to keep up with ever changing standards, or standards that were practical in a past time with different sets of circumstances. Fear of failure is a driving force, that is the thought of failing in someone else's eyes, or the fear of not living up to our own or someone's high expectations. Concern around failing is not a happy and fulfilling way to live our lives.

The truth is, if your child can be the authentic being it was created to be, expressing it's gifts, and having a fulfilling and rich life doing what he or she likes, contributing something they are good at in their own particular way, then your child has achieved success beyond measure. You have achieved beyond measure.

AFFIRMATIONS
MY MIND IS CLEAR
I AM INTELLIGENT
I HAVE THE RIGHT TO ASK FOR INFORMATION

CASE STUDY 1

Kathy is a woman of 29, who has recently been separated from her husband, Michael. She chose pale yellow/pale pink. Michael left her, and has a relationship with one of her close girlfriends. Kathy is full of stress, and concerned about her work and her life. She said she has lost not only her husband, but also a friend. She said she is fearful of the future, and wakes up every morning with anxiety.

Kathy feels rejected and unloved and her mind is overloaded with conflicts. She is glad the marriage is over, because they were often arguing, and yet she is uncertain. Kathy is going round and around in her mind, trying to find answers for how the marriage could have been different, and maybe she should have done more for Michael, and maybe he should have done more for her. She is confused and mentally exhausted.

Kathy wants to forgive Michael and her friend, Louise. Kathy said she feels heavy as though she is carrying a weight around in her mind. She has gone from being a happy and spontaneous person, to someone who is apprehensive and confused. She is seeing the world as a fearful place.

We spoke about Kathy's right to have her feelings, and the normality of feeling anger and apprehension at the changes in her life. She was well aware of needing to forgive Michael and Louise, and after we discussed it, she could see that forgiving them is a decision she can make for herself. Forgiveness would give her emotional closure. She can then say 'it has happened, it is over, and I won't keep going over it in my mind trying to find answers'.

We spoke about the power of the mind, and how she can see the situation in a new light. The situation will not change, but her attitude to it certainly can, and she gained freedom by her different perceptions. In this way, forgiveness is an act of love for herself, and she deserves that. When thoughts would come up that would create regret, she could acknowledge them and move on, rather than linger and go around in circles in her head.

Kathy could see her stress levels decreasing day by day with her new attitude, and the weight on her shoulders dropped away. Kathy had been married quite young, and had always wanted to study. She dropped any idea of this during her marriage as Michael always told her she was stupid.

Kathy came to see that it did not matter what Michael thought about her intelligence. She told herself she could learn, and when she was insecure or concerned Kathy focused on her affirmations, and the support they gave her. She chose the affirmations "I am intelligent", "I have the right to ask for information", and "I am lovable".

CASE STUDY 2

Sharon is in her thirties, and divorced from her second husband Greg. She chose yellow/blue.

Sharon said that she is 'over' men, and yet she is very lonely living a single life, and wonders why men don't treat her right, and call her a 'control freak'. Sharon grew up in a family where she was regarded by her father as a princess. She said there is no man in the world quite like her father, Roger, and certainly the two husbands she has had could not live up to being the man he was. The only man she ever trusted was her father, and she depended on him for everything.

As Sharon's story unfolded, she said she was the first to admit that Roger has spoilt her, because she was given every material thing she wanted. She only had to ask, and Roger was quick to comply. Sharon's mother, Meg, did not come into the picture in disciplining Sharon who so easily played her parents off against one another. In fact, she was not disciplined at all. Sharon knew she was more important to Roger than Meg.

When things did not go her way in the family as a child, Sharon would throw a tantrum. And this is what she did in both her marriages when her husbands did not attend to her every need. As Sharon described it, if they truly cared about her they would see it her way and give her what she wanted. Roger doted on Sharon and led her to believe that she could not trust herself without him, a blue issue. Sharon liked to be in control in the marriages, a possibility in yellow.

As we discussed the colours, Sharon came to realise the impact of her control and demands, on both her marriages, and that she needed to let go of controlling others, and trust herself. Over time Sharon learned to meet her own needs, and understand that relationships are give and take, not only take. In fact the more she developed a mature perception of her situations, the more she wanted to do with her life.

The affirmation Sharon selected was "I trust myself".

CHAPTER 11
OLIVE GREEN

Olive Green contains yellow and blue.

Olive is the tenderness and power of the heart. Olive shows a tenderhearted child. Olive is loyal and consistent, and offers a ray of hope when all seems lost.

Olive has the possibility of opening to the fullness of life. Physically the heart is essential to life as the beating of the heart keeps us alive; if your heart is not beating you won't live. Emotionally, if your heart is closed to the fullness of life, you don't really live. You merely exist.

Olive shows constancy and endurance, and the courage to overcome defeat or dejection.

Olive can be about letting go of pain in the heart. It can be about optimism, and allowing the light in your heart to shine out. Sometimes however, it indicates a sense of hopelessness.

Olive illustrates empowerment through your own truth. Of combining strength and vulnerability, force and gentleness.

Perhaps olive reveals a time of transition, of re-assessment and redefining one's true path.

Because olive has possibilities of heart issues, it may reveal someone who is emotionally discouraged and afraid to move on. Or it can be someone who is openhearted and willing to risk again.

Olive says, 'expand'; 'stretch beyond any perceived limitation'; 'make a leap of faith and believe in yourself'; 'come out of seclusion and move into your potentiality'. Olive says, 'trust the inner knowing of your heart'.

We are reminded by olive that everyone needs to receive nurturing as well as to give it, and that it is okay to ask for support. Olive offers you support, and suggests taking time for yourself when you need to be restored and revived, or where there are situations of exhaustion and depletion. Olive says your needs are important.

In essence, olive has generosity of spirit and is genuinely well intentioned. There is a gracefulness about olive which upholds the value of others.

Olive offers a definition of purpose and affirms your skills, capacity and unique characteristics. Olive says honour who you are, your truth.

Olive indicates an opportunity for releasing bitterness and betrayal from the heart. Like the olive that is pressed to extract any impurities leaving the pure essence of its oil, so the heart may be set free to return to its natural pure state.

Olive may show separation anxiety and fear of change, or reaffirming the deepest desires and moving in a new direction.

Olive could be a choice point, a time of liberation from any former oppressive beliefs held in a dis-empowering script. Olive supports you in learning to live again, with a revised affirming script which engenders hope for the future.

Olive can reveal leadership expressed as power with others, rather than power over others. With the heart as a guide, olive expresses strength and self-assurance in a peaceful way. Olive leads by example.

Although olive individuals do not always desire to distinguish themselves from the crowd, they have a certain presence, and could wield considerable influence. Olive can be silent and powerful at the same time.

Olive can herald new plans, and an opportunity to learn from the past. The existence of the past cannot be changed, but your attitude towards it can. Olive says life is an opportunity for the gift of growth and development. Take a step, have confidence in your heart's intuition.

Olive is like a soothing balm, offering caring from the heart.

Olive has a sense of camaraderie and is aware of the need to combine the individual strengths and resources of those in a group. Olive understands the importance of co-operation, and the effective force there is in strength of numbers. Olive encourages bonding with others for mutual support, and the common good. Olive upholds others and enjoys living in harmonious synthesis, where each individual recognises their potential and values, and contributes these for all to share equally. The undeveloped olive is competitive and jealous of the gifts and success of others.

Olive has a kind heart, offering reinforcement to those it perceives as overwhelmed, beaten and without recourse. Olive says you can overcome past limitations and step into the future believing that your life has meaning.

Olive encourages you to express your essential qualities, to leave uniformity behind, and come into your personal ownership, your integrity.

Olive says release burdensome thoughts, the 'what-if', 'if-only', and choices of the past. Olive asks 'is fear motivating your choices?' Olive says, 'it is the integrity with which you make choices, so trust your heart's guidance and choose honesty over dishonesty'.

Olive reminds us that nothing from the past is irretrievably lost; on the contrary everything is stored and treasured, and nobody can remove your gifts. The reason we look at the past is not to blame, but maybe there are unresolved issues that are keeping us stagnant. If the past is unresolved in the present, the future is likely to repeat the past.

Olive says, 'release yourself from regrets and tribulations of the heart: all is not lost; cherish what remains.' Olive indicates that with former events in our lives, we have a choice whether we pick these up and carry them around every day in the future. We can choose to reassess, and learn how to live again with fresh eyes.

Olive is perceptive and insightful, and can express the fullness and depth of feelings.

Olive recognises the power of a heart filled with gratitude.

Olive suggests beginnings and endings, unfolding and extending. Life may be seen as cycles of growth, and release. With olive we can become reconciled to the events of life, and the hearts potential for renewal.

AFFIRMATIONS
IT IS SAFE TO OPEN MY HEART
I AM FULL OF HOPE
MY LIFE IS EXPANDING AND UNFOLDING

CASE STUDY

Heather a 25 year old woman was very distressed and having difficulties with Irene her superior at work. She chose pale olive green/pink. Irene was 43, unmarried and very competitive. She made work her life, and had no time for social activities.

Heather's experience at work every day was that whatever she did, Irene would find fault. There seemed to be no way to please her. Irene would invade the workspace of Heather, looking through papers, reading her mail and Heather said Irene was constantly looking over her shoulder. Heather felt watched.

Irene told Heather the only way to be successful was to outwit everyone else, and there was no point in being soft and feminine. Being kind hearted would get you nowhere in the world and she would never open her heart to anyone. She had been betrayed too many times to let anyone into her heart or her life; possibilities found in pink and olive.

This was the total opposite of the beliefs and qualities of Heather, and yet she started to doubt herself being with Irene so much. Heather found it very difficult to be with Irene all day at work, and yet she loved the job itself, and did not want to leave. She was beginning to feel hopeless, and unable to express her truth, what was she to do? She was experiencing dejection and oppression.

Heather needed to use the gifts of pink and olive, and really listen to herself and follow her heart's intuition. She began to see that she had the courage to overcome the stagnation that had settled in this job. She changed her beliefs about herself as being powerless and ineffective in this situation, and saw it as an opportunity for growth and affirming her essential truth. Heather came to see herself as a human being with worth and potential.

She could express to Irene her heartfelt truth without expectations of the outcome, or wanting Irene to change. By Heather making these changes to her sense of self, Irene came to view her with respect. Heather understood that by changing her perception of the situation, she had a sense of personal empowerment. She needed to listen to her own needs, and support herself, showing kindness and caring when she needed it.

The affirmation she chose to use was "My life is expanding and unfolding".

CHAPTER 12
EMERALD GREEN

Emerald Green contains blue and yellow

Emerald Green is about renewal, so it can be renewal of life or renewal of direction. Green can suggest a need to move on. Green could indicate making decisions about new beginnings, taking a new path in life, a new direction. Emerald Green asks, 'Where am I, and where do I want to go?' Emerald Green is about growth and change, and our responses to them.

Green can have difficulty with decisions, when often deep inside they know, but they cannot choose. Green says when you are stuck around decisions, follow your heart. Green reminds you that you are enough as you are.

Emerald Green children are generous, open hearted, and truthful. Green people are friendly. Green is about renewal, so it can be renewal of life or renewal of direction. Green can be about taking time for yourself, and making time for friendships.

Green can have difficulty with decisions, when often deep inside they know, but they cannot choose. Green says when you are stuck around decisions, follow your heart. Green can indicate a need to move on. Green says to remember you are enough as you are. Green could indicate making decisions about new beginnings, taking a new path in life, a new direction, asking, 'Where am I, and where do I want to go?'

Green says apprehension is a natural feeling accompanying new beginnings. Commencing a new job, even when the new one is right, can trigger some anxiety. Likewise a new relationship even if the relationship is good, or a new school, a new residence, or a new chapter in our lives. At these times there is a need to let go and trust this new experience, with the risk of vulnerability it brings. Green says we can learn to trust new beginning, trust movement, trust change, and open our hearts and lives.

Green says to remember that life is full of choices. Each day is full of many choice points and you can choose in any given moment for another option. Whatever your map of the world, whatever your script, when you learn another path you can take it, whenever you choose. You can shift into your real values at any time. Sometimes the new path will seem easier and full of possibilities, sometimes harder and full of uncertainties and the unknown. Children live with the unknown everyday. They live with this vulnerability as they learn so much and grow and change.

Some changes are quick and relatively easy, and some take more practice, so we need to be patient with ourselves. When we are learning, some things take more time. Take heart, because often what it takes us longer to learn we remember for a longer time. Remember that when a child learns to walk they often fall over and there may be a few tears, maybe a few bruises, but the child can get up again and keep trying to walk, trying to hold the balance. Then comes that moment when they can do it automatically, when they can walk, and there is a sense of empowerment. So now they have learned to walk, and mastered it, there are other steps to take in their growth, maybe they want to ride a bike, fly a kite, ski, eventually drive a car, and they practice till they learn it, and master that too. As adults we can feel childlike when we are learning something new as part of our growth and expansion. Green suggests that instead of criticising yourself when you fall over, congratulate yourself on taking the risk of learning, changing, and growing. Be as gentle with yourself as you would with a child who fell over while trying to learn something new.

Green can indicate openness and generosity, or, alternatively, it can indicate holding onto money, and possessions.

Green has an expansive open quality, or a sense of needing more space, more room, more freedom. Green is the doorway to freedom, a step in a new direction. Do you have a need for space and freedom in your life? Lovers of their own space and freedom do not like to be cramped in relationships or work. Green can suggest envy or jealousy, or wanting to be in the space of another.

Green can reveal issues to do with the heart, an open heart, or a heart closed because of hurt, and the inability or anxiety to trust anew. Green is often about harmony or the need for it, about change, rejuvenation and expansion or the need for decisions regarding these. Certainly green indicates people of integrity who are honest and open, or have the need for this in their lives. Green can reveal a broken heart, with a need for renewal of life. Green has lots of feelings in the heart, and maybe some of them need to be expressed.

Green illustrates that in group situations, or in the presence of another, there is a need for personal boundaries. Often because of their deeply feeling nature, green does not always know which feelings are theirs, or which feelings are those of another.

Green is straightforward and to the point and often wonders why other people are not. Green indicates heart-felt honest people, direct in their communication who perhaps believed it was not safe to speak honestly. Green people may be needing a new direction in their method of communication. Perhaps it is time for new growth in this area. Green shows optimism.

Green can often be about comparing and being compared. A child can perceive itself as the one who is not the favourite in the family, not the attractive one, not the intelligent one, not the one who excels, not the one favoured by the mother or father, or at school. They can adopt an attitude that they are less- than, and take this into the world with them, into their school, into college, into their relationships, into their work, into social situations, and this belief can cloud who they really are and their prospects for a fulfilling life.

A child can feel neglected because they do not get the time and attention they need, and so they believe they are less important than whatever does get the time and attention. For example they can feel less important than the work of the father, than another child, than the activities of the mother which keep her preoccupied, than the interests of the father which keep him absent or too busy for them. There are many situations where a child feels "less than", and these are just a few examples. It is reasonable for a child to have feelings about these situations. Often they are unable to express these feelings, which subsequently get locked in and can carry over into adulthood. They compare themselves to others, and then because they come from a "less than" position in their lives, many adults can feel inadequate in friendships, relationships, in social situations, and at work. Often they then try to compensate by acting "more than", with unpleasant consequences.

Is the child in fear of the father because he is a remote figure who only sees them briefly when he is not working? When this happens the child often feels less-than what seems more important to the father. This gives children early concepts about work. Perhaps they will want to be good at work to be like their father, or go the absolute opposite, and believe there is nothing I can do to be as good, as important, as brave, as competent, as intelligent, as successful, as my father, older brother, mother, uncle, teacher, etc. This becomes their perception of the world and their place in it.

Green is about new beginnings, movement and going somewhere. It is also the opposite of this, a sense of being immobilised, stuck, unable to decide and going nowhere. What to do when we get stuck? Green suggests you try this, to get you moving. Make the decision to move, and the step of this small decision can make the space for something to happen. Green says, 'just this small step, is a step in the right direction for you; you have made a choice.' Say to yourself, 'this is my life, and these are my values, my choices, what I want for my life'. Look at a value you are working with, or would like to work with and take a step with that. Ask 'Which of my values, my stars, will I call on when I am stuck?' Remember you are okay as you are right now. You have always been okay, and will always be okay just the way you are. So you have made a shift, your energy has gone out in a direction of your choice, instead of being stuck in the way of the past.

Green says, 'know your truth for yourself, feel your heart, what is it saying to you?'; 'What is your truth?' Green can show a cheerful anticipation of the future.

AFFIRMATIONS
I AM SAFE TO STEP IN A NEW DIRECTION
THERE IS TIME FOR ME
I ACCEPT MYSELF AS I AM

CASE STUDY 1

Annette a 32 year old woman was presently experiencing anxiety in her life. She chose green/blue. She felt stifled and wanted a change of direction, and had fear at making the wrong decision. Annette could see she did not want to continue living her life for other people the way she had in the past. She wanted to start living for herself and to fulfill her heart's desire.

Annette was a very nervous person who had great difficulty with decisions. She believed that whatever she did it would not be right, so she became stuck, and had a sense of apprehension when a new direction, or change was imminent. Her life had been a series of stops and starts and indecision.

Annette often did not want to meet people because she had developed a fear of not knowing how to express herself, and did not say anything for fear of making the wrong choice about what to say. Annette said she was often lost for words, and could not remember facts that were well known to her. She would become confused and tongue-tied.

Annette lived with her parents and would like to leave, move to a new area, and live alone for the first time in her life. This desire was very strong, and yet each time she thought about it, she would be filled with apprehension, and not want to leave the house at all.

She was a deeply feeling child, whose father Sean was absent much of the time on business, and when he was home he did not speak. Her mother Nicole took the dominating role in the family, and she was angry most of the time. Unfortunately for Annette, Nicole had a violent temper which she would express as constant criticism of her daughter. This left Annette believing she could never do anything right or say the right things, so she would not speak at all.

Annette did not ever feel safe in the family home with her mother, and she had no idea how to talk to her father. This left her living a life of isolation and uncertainty. She expressed feeling cramped living with her mother, but Annette was uncertain what it was like in the world on her own. It was as if she had a love/hate relationship with Nicole, who was jealous of Annette.

Annette had a sense that it was 'now or never', and that if she did not move soon, she would be confined with her parents and this to her was like a prison sentence. She was having difficulty trusting herself.

When Annette was stuck, I suggested she take small steps, and make simple decisions to begin to give her confidence and learn to trust herself. The first step was to make the mental decision to move. Taking this tiny step gave her a sense of power that she could decide for herself. This is a step in the right direction for her as she had made a simple choice.

Annette learned she needed to remember to say to herself, 'just a moment', and take time out. The action of this thought, would give her time to step back, take a few deep breaths, and calm down. From this more peaceful place, her thinking became calmer and Annette was in a position to decide slowly. When necessary she would affirm to herself: 'Remember you are okay as you are right now. You have always been okay, and will always be okay just the way you are.'

Annette was judgmental of herself and needed to understand that she was okay the way she was. She would become indecisive, and judge herself for being indecisive, then this would send her into a deeper spiral of indecision. At these times, she would stop, and remember a value on her Startree. This step of stopping what she was thinking about, and replacing it with the thought of something that had meaning and value to her, broke her old pattern of criticism and self-judgements. Using the values on her Startree was an extremely valuable exercise for Annette who practiced affirming to herself many times a day, 'this is my life, and these are my values, my choices, and what I want for my life.'

She needed to take the step of expressing herself to people and trusting that sometimes people will agree with her, and sometimes they won't. Sometimes people will like her and sometimes they won't. This is a fact of life. And that difference in thinking is valuable, not detrimental. People are all different, and will naturally think differently, so Annette saw that difference is a positive and not a negative thing. She learned that what she can do is trust speaking her truth from the heart, and not to agree with everything that is said to keep the peace, gifts of green and blue.

Annette learned that some changes are relatively quick and easy, and some take longer. She learned to be gentle with herself, and celebrate each small decision she made. As Annette gained confidence with the small everyday decisions, the bigger decisions could be made. So it was a step by step process. She chose the affirmations "I trust myself with decisions" and "I am safe to express my truth".

CASE STUDY 2

John, a 34 year old man with two children is stressed out from working and the time spent commuting to work each day, and struggling to keep his marriage together. He chose pale green/pale green. His wife complained that he did not spend enough time with her, and he believed he had no time to himself.

John needed to discuss his life and come to some peaceful space where his heart was not cramped in his chest from stress. He said he had taken to drinking alcohol to ease his stress, but found the results of this in his life increased his stress, and did not ease the problem. The drinking became part of the problem and not part of the solution.

John wondered if this was his fate forever. He was not optimistic about his future, which he perceived as only work and never to have time for himself. He said he felt envy of those with a better life than he had.

He said as a child he was the only boy of three children, and he was expected to care for others and he knew his parents had no time for him with other smaller children, and so he had no experience of having time for his needs. John was constantly compared to his father and did not measure up. He was expected to be a man when he was a child. Whatever he did he believed was not enough and this put him under enormous stress to try to do more and more.

In his family the males were not encouraged to have their heart or feelings, and in fact John is a person with an open generous heart who felt some shame around having such depth of feelings. He thought drinking with his male friends from work would show his masculinity, but deep within there was the belief he was 'less than' and inferior in some way.

John found relief in knowing he was perfect the way he was created, and he could be easier on himself once he understood he did not come from a less than position. John had never experienced being acknowledged for the individual he was, and that his feelings mattered and that he was not merely to exist for the good of others. Because he had only experienced life from a less than position, he was always trying to achieve or do something to find a sense that he was enough. He was repeating the pattern of his childhood where he was always expected to 'be a man'. How does a child know what this means? They are left trying to be more than they are, and not sure how to be that.

John's life experience had been 'I should achieve more, earn more, work longer hours, and give my wife and children more', and the stress and pressure had become intolerable. All the time he had he gave to others, exactly like his childhood, where his parents expected this, and they had no time for him. He had not learned it is necessary to have time for himself.

We discussed John's levels of stress and how he could use time management to find some space for himself with his busy schedule. He needed time out. We developed a series of breathing exercises he could do at work or on the train. If he closed his eyes he could focus on his breathing, and sense that with every breath out he was releasing his tension, and letting go of the tightness in his chest. The idea was that every breath out gave him the opportunity of becoming calmer. As he was focusing on his breathing, with his eyes gently closed, he could imagine a peaceful place in nature, such as a mountain or by a river, and sense himself there, and he found that with practice his breathing would slow down. When thoughts came into his mind, he could let them drift by like clouds.

With practice, John could do these exercises with more ease, and the more he did them, the more his stress levels decreased. He could do these stress releasing exercises in breaks at work, or travelling on the train which he previously found relentlessly boring and a waste of time. Instead of getting more stressed on the train, he arrived at work and at home in a much less tense mood. He used this time to his advantage, and benefitted not only himself but his family and work associates. John wanted his heart to be open and free, and he could gain a sense of this, by using this time out exercise. He was experiencing more inner and outer equilibrium and harmony, qualities among the gifts of green.

John realised the drinking sessions after work were not a solution or what he needed, so he could make choices about when and with whom he wanted to spend his time. He did not need to compete or compare himself with others. John moved into a place of being able to decide when he could take this time for himself, all green issues. He chose to work with the affirmations "I am taking time for myself", "My heart is open and free", and "I am enough as I am".

CHAPTER 13
TURQUOISE

Turquoise contains blue and yellow.

Turquoise can be bright, progressive and idealistic. Turquoise offers friendship for no personal advantage, and is generally benevolent to everyone. Particularly in children, turquoise is insightful and helpful.

Turquoise seeks to align itself with the highest human qualities, and aspires towards the greatest benefits for all. Turquoise stands for humanitarian liberation, the spirit of goodwill

Turquoise could be shy, reticent, and reserved, or have some challenges around self-expression. Often turquoise people express themselves through creativity or artistic pursuits, for example, designing, writing, painting, drawing, music, or dance.

Sometimes perceived as stoic, a turquoise person can be someone who is shut off, and has problems expressing their inner world.

The undeveloped turquoise is liable to be abrasive and disregarding of feelings, their own and those of others. They could choose to involve themselves with technology, rather than become involved with relationships, and perhaps lack interpersonal skills.

Turquoise offers the opportunity to bring forth the true you. Turquoise asks 'do you feel appreciated for who you really are?'; 'who am I and what am I here for?' Turquoise says 'search inside and acknowledge your own distinctive spark; listen to your inner guidance'; 'it is time to share and express your individual truth and know this is okay.'

Turquoise could indicate a lack of self-trust in matters of the heart. In this situation, there are emotions they would like to express, but somehow these are blocked. Turquoise inquires, 'is there more you would like to express, to contribute?'

Often enjoying electronics, a turquoise person is frequently adept at computers, expressing himself or herself through this medium. The downside of this is they have more of a relationship with the computer, than they have with other human beings. In the case of an adult turquoise, this can damage primary relationships, and the building of a social network. With children, they do not learn how to interact and form friendships. Children need to bond to someone, ideally, parents, family and peers. If this is not possible, they bond with something, for instance, a computer, and subsequently they do not learn social tools or experience warm human interactions.

Turquoise stirs us out of our complacency, and can herald change and the unexpected. Turquoise people may be seen as unusual in thought, speech or action. They can be exciting and slightly unnerving, for one is not always sure what some turquoise individuals will do next.

Some turquoise are talkative, while others struggle to put their thoughts into words. This causes a sense of loneliness, or being separate. Turquoise says, 'do not isolate or hold back.'

Turquoise says, 'appreciate your individual attributes'; 'all of us are different, all unique'; 'we are created this way.' And each individual is special. In which ways are you different? Turquoise inspires you to have the courage to be yourself, and then the need for approval falls away.

Turquoise suggests individual creativity is essential in finding solutions to the changing world, and helping us look where no one ever looked before.

Turquoise is liberal and receptive. It can illustrate flexibility, or the need for this.

There is the likelihood turquoise reveals someone who is effervescent and uplifting. The other side can be an individual who is distant and withholds from personal revelation.

The undeveloped turquoise could be a daydreamer who lives in a fantasy world, and does not venture to communicate. Turquoise suggests that you make the decision for your life to be more than fantasies and wishful thinking. Turquoise says, 'uncover your originality and contribute that'; 'share with each other.'

Turquoise may be sympathetic, well intentioned and humane, or emotionally cool and restrained.

Turquoise offers the opportunity to become aware of the words you use, and how you feel as you say and hear them. The words that make you feel good when you say them to yourself. If you notice yourself feeling anxious or depressed, be creative with your thinking and use words that make you feel better. So what are the creative words which encourage you to feel better? What would you like to create in your day? If you would normally be critical, create something else. Create praise. What would you like?

Turquoise suggests you spend time thinking about what you want, rather than what you don't want. If you are around someone or in a situation and you feel your confidence slipping away, be creative and recall a helpful value, or think of a word that will uplift you. No one is inside your head but you, and within this context you can create whatever you choose. Maybe that is hope, optimism, peace and love. Or confidence, by believing you can.

When asked, 'How do I conduct my life with meaning, express myself, and have a fulfilling life', turquoise answers, 'Use your Startree values to make a difference, say what is in your heart', and 'trust your inner knowing.'

AFFIRMATIONS
MY HEART IS NOW FREE
I HAVE THE RIGHT TO EXPERIENCE AND EXPRESS MY FEELINGS
I AM CREATIVE AND TALENTED

CASE STUDY

Noel, a 23-year-old man was very close to his father who died four years ago of a stroke. Noel chose turquoise/violet. Noel and his father Jack had very good communication, and after Jack had the stroke he was like a vegetable and Noel had far to travel to visit him in hospital. Each time he visited the hospital, Noel hoped for a miracle, and that his father would return once more to what he was. Noel felt shut off from his father and the talks they shared, and disliked seeing his father this way. He believed he had never said goodbye to his father, and he wished that he had.

Since Jack died, Noel lives alone with his mother and does not talk at all. He believes he has not really spoken to anyone since his father died and the loneliness is extremely difficult.

Noel believes no one understands him, and he does not trust himself to speak to others and ask for support or share how he feels. He expressed feeling regretful if he spoke to anyone.

Noel had some difficulty describing his feelings at the time of his father's death. He had pushed his feelings down because he thought it was not manly. He believed he should not speak of his concern to his mother.

We spoke of the need of every person whether male or female, to express their feelings, and not to lock them deep inside. To help him with his regrets about the unspoken words at the time of his father death and the grief, I suggested he write a letter to his father saying whatever he wished he had said, and he could read it out aloud to me, if he chose to. I believed Noel needed to express himself with someone, and with me it was the first step.

Noel wanted to tell his father he was sorry he didn't like going to the hospital, that it was painful to see him and yet know he could not speak to him when he was so ill. He said he did not want to go to the hospital, not because he didn't want to see his father, but because he did not like to see his father this way. He said how he had hoped for a miracle, and was angry when one did not occur.

Noel wrote that he missed the talks they had shared since his childhood, and that the thought that they would never do this again was overwhelmingly sad. He told his father how deeply lonely he was, and the loneliness was like a void where he was utterly alone and unheard. Noel also wrote and told his father about his life now, what is happening and what he wants to happen in the future.

The need to express is very deep in turquoise, so Noel was an individual to whom communication was a very necessary part of his life. I explained it is necessary for every human being to express pain at the loss of a loved one (violet), and he was relieved to know this was okay for men.

Noel chose to work with the affirmation "I am healing now", "It is safe to express my feelings", and "I am safe and protected".

CHAPTER 14
BLUE

Blue is about communication and expressing opinions, thoughts or needs, even if these are different to others. Do you want to speak and have your voice? Do you need to ask for something? Being with undeveloped blue can give you a sense that they are not going to tell you what they want, but they expect you to read their mind.

Blue is about serenity, trust, faith and doubt. Where you have faith you have the possibility of doubt, as they are two sides of the same coin. Doubt is an opportunity for faith and trust.

Peace is significant for blue individuals, and they strive towards the ideal of peace with a purpose. In craving peace they often keep silent in order to have a peaceful life. The experience of this can be that you want to speak and express what you think, but don't because you want to keep the peace. Consequently your own inner peace is sacrificed, and often the price you pay is your peace of mind.

Blue speaks of loyalty, duty, dedication, and devotion. Blue brings a sense of contentment, and asks 'Are you content?' Blue can be reflective, a dreamer. Blue speaks of nurturing. Children need to be nurtured and protected, and to know it is safe to be who they are.

They need to be taught to have faith in themselves, and yet they are often not nurtured and encouraged to be their true colours. Blue children need to be taught to communicate and express their difference, and trust this. Children need to learn that they are not their role, school marks, work, clothes, figure, or achievements. They need to trust that their importance does not lie with what they do, or what they accomplish, or what they own, or their degrees, or how they look or don't look, or whether they are married or not, but to trust that they are important because they were born and they are individuals. Blue needs to express its difference to the world. Blue says 'trust yourself, and reveal your individual qualities'.

Blue can have a sense of tranquility and inner calm. Those working with blue may like to go off quietly on their own, or think things through. Blue is about honour and allegiance. Blue individuals are pacifists. Their gift of conciliation makes them excellent mediators.

Blue can indicate a child who had no one there to talk to and trust with his or her thoughts. This can lead to adults who will not share what they think. Blue may indicate perhaps a lack of attention from the mother, or maybe a passive father and dominating mother, or possibly a remote father or mother, and this can lead to lack of trust in authority figures. Children are aware of the unspoken in families and can feel it is their responsibility to replace dad for mum; to take care of mum when dad is not there, or to nurture mum so she can look after the children when she believes her life is not valuable, because women are viewed by some people as less than men are. Those working with blue have often become the parent to their parent.

Children need attention and if the adult is unavailable to a child, it may try to get the attention any way it can, to ease the sense of isolation it is experiencing. To a child, even negative attention is better than no attention. He or she can behave badly, or get sick, or fail, or rebel. This is not who the child is, it is their behaviour.

Boys selecting blue may not want to spend their lives achieving, and following the male role model of father or husband as described to them by society, or as expressed through the media. They may desire to contribute their uniqueness in different ways, and then struggle because they feel they will be letting down their family, their mother, their father, or their teacher. Children have the right to be affirmed and supported to be who they are without having to live up to the expectations of another. They have the right to acceptance just because they exist, not because they achieve recognition in some way for the family or school. Just because they exist. This is an unusual concept for some, who believe the family or group is more important than the individual. It does not imply chaos, or that the family is not important. It implies valuing our children for who they are and not expecting and wanting them to be like us; to support them to have their own true colours, and contribute their uniqueness.

As I discussed in Chapter 1, children are not responsible for the unfulfilled ambitions and dreams of their parents or grandparents, but have the right to their individuality and the expression of their uniqueness.

Every individual is entitled to their likes and dislikes, and often we don't know what we really like because we haven't realised that we have the right to express our thoughts – blue issues. We believe we like something because we have been told it is 'right'. The right kind of husband, the right kind of wife, the right kind of job, the right kind of clothes, the right degree, the right friends, the right haircut, the right music, the right image, the right education, the right age, the right gender, the right school, the right university, the right behaviour. In some circles, a person's worth depends on these 'right' things. However, the truth is that a child has worth because it was born. There is always room for traditional values, and for these to be expressed by the individual. Children can have a different haircut, choice of job, wear different clothes, like a different kind of music, be interested in different subjects, have different thoughts, and still hold many traditional values dear to their heart.

World famous individuals like Albert Einstein, Mozart, or Michelangelo, thought differently and they gave to the world by the expression of their individuality. They were assuredly different, and all contributed uniquely. And so does the person who is a shop assistant, a street sweeper, an office worker, a bus driver, a chef, a student, or a housewife. The contributions of every individual whether seen in the eyes of another as great or small, are important. Everyone is valuable.

Blue says nurture children, guide them with love, support them to talk and express themselves while being interested and paying attention to what they say and think. This shows them that what they think, and feel, and want to say, matters.

Blue offers the opportunity of assuming our personal power, and trusting ourselves to communicate our thoughts and values. Blue can feel safe, or unsafe; alone, or all one. Do you feel appreciated for who you really are? Do you feel sure of who you really are? Do you believe there is a part inside you that is waiting to come alive and be expressed in your life? Do you sense that there could be more to your life, more to communicate, more to contribute? Blue inspires you to nurture yourself, encourage yourself every step of the way, and move at your own pace. Blue says, 'trust the process of life, and do not be attached to outcomes'; 'trust that the right thing will happen at the right time.'

Blue tends to communicate in one of three ways, by moving closer and talking things over, by moving away and going silent and withdrawn, or moving against and verbally counter attacking. Blue asks, 'how do you choose to communicate?'

Blue can speak of issues about the father and the implications from childhood through to adulthood. A distant father teaches us to find someone who is unattainable or does not notice us. The doting father may keep you dependent on him, indicating you are unable to trust yourself without him. The absent father through death, divorce, desertion, or heavy work commitments, speaks of a reluctance to trust a man to stay with you. A domineering father teaches you not to speak up, it is not safe to talk. An inappropriate father is liable to leave the child with the belief, 'do not trust'.

The absence of fathering during childhood affects each person differently. Some blue children can spend their life searching for a father, someone to take care of them, and seek that in a husband. Unfortunately, very often the child can grow into an adult who repeats the pattern by having a partner who is not there for you, who has more important things than you in their life, so sustaining the belief that you have adopted.

Beliefs can be changed. It is never too late. There are beliefs that may be more appropriate to another age, another set of circumstances. It is a choice. There can come a time when an early belief has come to an end or an old emotional concept does not fit. Children are learning new concepts all the time as they grow and change. In a world that is changing everyday, we as adults have the need and capacity to do the same.

'What is my life for and am I leading it the way that is best?' 'What am I here for?' 'What will I offer?' Keys to this may be found in your colours and values. Trust yourself and if you have a dream go for it. If you believe there is more of you to be expressed, go for it. Trust yourself. It can be done, and you can do it. Follow your star, the star of who you really are.

Blue says you can encounter many defeats, and still not be defeated.

Blue speaks of faith in ourselves, and our higher purpose.

AFFIRMATIONS
I HAVE FAITH IN THE PROCESS OF MY LIFE
I TRUST MYSELF
I AM SAFE TO SPEAK

CASE STUDY 1

Ruth, a 17-year-old teenager was having great difficulties due to the fact that her parents had divorced when she was young. She chose blue/blue. She became the companion to her mother, mixing primarily with adults.

Ruth was seemingly mature for her age, and yet experienced great difficulty trusting anyone, particularly males, and trusting herself. She expressed having many thoughts going around in her head, but did not want to say anything in case she was not understood.

When we discussed the colour blue, Ruth began to recognise the deeper impact of her father leaving Ruth alone with her mother. She needed to understand that her father wanted the divorce from her mother, he did not want to divorce Ruth. It was not Ruth's fault, and there was nothing she could do to stop him leaving them. This impact accounted for her lack of trust in males. Ruth expressed beliefs of 'if I trust you, will you leave me?'

Because in effect, she became the companion for her mother to ease mother's loneliness, Ruth could not complete her childhood, and had a pseudo-adultness about her. This can happen with children who are expected to be older than they are, where they become like 'pretend adults'.

Ruth experienced an inner loneliness, and said that while she was there for everyone else, no one was there for her. She did not want to say what she needed or felt in case she was 'too much', which was the echo of her childhood experience where neither of her parents were there for her.

Ruth expressed great relief at being able to tell her story, and begin to trust it was now safe to be herself. She did not have to 'act big', or try to be super-mature. And there was a relief that within the counselling environment Ruth could trust a female to be there for her, and she did not need to be the nurturer. She chose to work with the affirmations "I am safe to speak", and "I can now trust myself and others".

CASE STUDY 2

Jennifer, was in her thirties, a divorced woman with two teenage daughters, Rachel and Kathleen. Jennifer chose pale blue/pale pink.

She was feeling a great deal of stress and struggling in her life to say what she thought. She believed that she was misunderstood whenever she said anything, so why say anything at all. Jennifer was having conflict with her mother Bess about how to live her life, and how to raise two teenage girls.

Jennifer said she felt lonely inside, and wondered how she was going to cope. All she wanted in her life was some peace, and that it eluded her.

Jennifer was definite in her belief that she was not loved and accepted by Bess, and that she had a lot of challenges with her mother, who she saw as very strong, and in fact the dominant person in her family. Her father Bill did not say much at all, and she did not feel protected by him from her mother.

Jennifer realised she was expecting a husband to be a prince charming and take care of her, in the way she believed she needed as a child. She was now in the position of needing to take responsibility for her own needs, and those of her children Rachel and Kathleen, and was feeling lonely and depressed. She said if she shouted no one would hear her.

Because she has a combination of pale blue and pale pink, we needed to talk about both colours. She found through discussing blue, that the loneliness was an echo of her childhood, and that now she could trust herself to speak and express her needs and thoughts. After she began to talk, and find there was a meaning to her life, she was encouraged to have her inner personal power and express that. Jennifer found more peace of mind, and a sense of inner serenity that had been lacking.

With the pale pink there was a hidden frustration with her father Bill, and the knowledge that he could not hear her. She then projected this anger onto her husband, when he was not the man of her dreams, taking care of all her needs.

Jennifer's growth included listening to her own needs, and taking care of those, and being gentle with herself. By showing kindness and caring to herself, she was in more of a position to offer that to the children, without a sense that she was giving all this love out, and none was coming in.

The affirmations she chose to work with were "I am lovable and peaceful" and "I trust my personal power".

CHAPTER 15
ROYAL BLUE

Royal Blue contains blue and red.

Royal blue indicates individuals who are likely to be strong-minded. Royal blue thinks differently and may have the gift of expressing involved and profound concepts. Royal blue points to fluid conversation, or blocks in the flow of communication.

There could be a certain reserve and quiet calmness surrounding royal blue people. They may be at one with the universe, or feel utterly alone.

They are often intelligent people who become engrossed in their thoughts, which they may have difficulty articulating. This can cause the sense of isolation or loneliness. It may be experienced as, 'how do I communicate all that is in my head?' 'How can I explain what comes into my mind?' Frequently they have intuitive and conceptualized thinking, which others may not grasp. Royal blue can have hidden embarrassment or shame because they think differently, and don't want to express this. Perhaps they have not been understood when expressing the individual way they think, and so they don't trust or speak about it.

Royal blue suggests that you share your thoughts, intuitions and concepts with others, and trust that some people will understand you and some won't, and that is okay.

Others may perceive royal individuals as unfriendly, withdrawn or unsociable, when in fact the royal blue perception could be that they don't belong, or they are not always sure how to converse with people.

Royal blue can create a world in their mind. Royal blue asks, 'what world are you creating with your thoughts?' 'What are you saying to yourself about the situations in your life?' 'Do you see them as opportunities or failures?' With royal blue you can use your mind to challenge any negative perceptions of an outdated script. A negative belief that 'I can't trust others to love or nurture me' becomes a self-fulfilling prophecy, because in pushing others away, there is no one there to nurture you, no one to trust. Royal blue suggests you focus on positive aspects of yourself and your life, which means collecting evidence contrary to old thought patterns and scripts. Maybe at the beginning of each day you could review your Startree and values, and make choices for your script in line with your integrity.

Selecting royal blue reveals the likelihood of an individual who had to cope with authority shown to them that was without compassion. Or a person who was around an authority figure who had difficulty expressing kindness and caring. Perhaps there was someone who believed that authority should be 'over', and not 'with', and did not trust and encourage you to learn to trust yourself and your own thoughts and expression. Authority used as power 'over' is not a win/win situation; win/win respects the rights of others. Royal blue says, 'you can trust yourself to be an authority who genuinely cares, and contribute by expressing this.'

Royal blue can be either absolutely comfortable in a silent world, or experience confinement and restriction.

Royal blue people may be perceived as distant and cold, when actually they are often shy, private and quiet.

Trust and faith can be strong issues for those with royal blue, trusting it is safe to share the deeper levels of themselves with others. Royal blue inquires: 'do you feel lonely, very alone?' 'Do you feel you want someone to talk to, really talk to and share your thoughts and feelings?' 'Do you feel that if you talked no one would understand what you are saying, what you are meaning?' Royal blue asks, 'what is it you are not expressing?' 'Is there something you would like to say?' Royal blue says, 'you have the right to your inner world and feelings, and to communicate these'.

Royal blue says 'it is not your intellectual prowess that creates your value'. 'You are not your thoughts; you are more than your thoughts.' 'It does not matter whether you have a degree or diploma or not, you matter'.

The selection of royal blue may indicate an individual who feels overshadowed by a parent, even if the parent is dead. Royal blue may refer to a parent who still wants to have authority and dominance over their child. Royal blue suggests that when a child is grown and having their life, it is time to cut the umbilical cord. We can trust they will know what is right for them.

Because royal blue individuals have a private world of their own and keep to themselves, they could be viewed by others as unapproachable and aloof. However inside, royal blue individuals may feel unwanted and singularly isolated.

There is the possibility that royal blue people may be distressed at feeling solitary, because they believe they are not the same as other people. Royal blue says, 'remember that if we were meant to be all the same, we would have been created that way'. We are created as individuals because that is what we have to offer to each other and the world, our difference, not our sameness. If we were meant to be all the same, we would have been created that way.

Royal blue suggests the need for trusting your values and purpose. Royal blue individuals may wonder, 'why am I here?' Royal blue says, 'we are here for a reason and each individual has something unique to offer the world'.

Royal blue reminds us that we are not alone, and our existence matters.

AFFIRMATIONS
I HAVE DEEP INNER PEACE
I HAVE THE RIGHT TO MY INDIVIDUALITY
I HAVE THE RIGHT TO MY THOUGHTS

CASE STUDY 1

Wendy is a 41-year-old woman, who had come to an impasse in her life. She selected royal blue/turquoise. She was working in a television station and was suffering from burnout, stress and frustration with her life situation.

She knew she was very strong and had believed she needed to defend herself against the world. It was as if she rushed headlong into everything, needing to fight and struggle to be successful. Her approach to life had been to lock horns with authority from the time she was very young, and whatever anyone in authority said to her, she wanted to do the opposite. If they said 'yes', she said 'no'. If they said 'no', she said 'yes'.

She was highly intelligent and articulate, and used words as batons and shield, and had found this effective, until now. She had lived a life of rebellion, thwarting authority wherever she could.

She was experiencing a sense that she was too tired to continue to live this way, always having battles and never believing she could find someone to trust. Even though she was successful, she had always felt isolated and alone, with a deep sense of mistrust at letting down her barriers.

Wendy was the second child, with an older sister. In families, very often the first child is the one who is encouraged to be the achiever, and gains value and esteem in the family by being 'good'. The second child cannot compete with this, and does not get attention for being 'good', so they get attention by going the other way. Better to get negative attention than no attention at all, so often they are rebellious, or sick. They can become the scapegoat in the family, the negative focus, and take the blame. If you are a scapegoat in your family for any reason, you will know it. Any child or adult who is the family scapegoat needs to be reassured around their personal value, and not to identify with their behaviour.

Wendy definitely identified with the role of scapegoat, and came to see that her life had been a repeat of the pattern she had with her father. She was at loggerheads with him from the time she was a small girl. He had no time for her, and thought she was a disgrace because she did not behave like her sister. Wendy saw that she gained attention from her father by being 'bad', and had in effect done the same thing with others. During her life a great deal of the time she really agreed with what was being said by men or others she perceived as authority figures, but something inside her compelled her to say the opposite.

Wendy knew she had a second sense about people, and could see this had developed as a child when she was around her highly critical father. She would sense when he was going to blame or reject her, and she jumped in first, misbehaved, and gave him something to reject her for. When she was a child, Wendy somehow protected herself from feeling rejection by behaving in a way that caused rejection, and it was the same in her life. She was intensely lonely because by believing she would be rejected, she behaved by pushing people away before they could get close. She had not learned to trust in her family, and she was not sure how to do that now. Her intense sense of isolation and loneliness at this point in her life was something she wanted to address. Wendy believed she could not go on the way she had been.

Wendy needed to understand that she was okay the way she was. In fact, how could she behave like her sister, when she was not her sister? How can one child be like another, when they are created differently because they have something different to offer the world.

We talked about her need to learn to trust that some people would understand and care for her, and some would not, and not to push people away by anticipating rejection. She knew this was what she had done in her life, and had many regrets about it. In fact she had been in and out of many relationships, and some she regretted leaving.

Wendy recognised that because of the relationship she had with her father and her sister, she tried to compete with men and women. Her competition would take the form of expressing disagreement with opinions which were offered, and always taking an opposition stance.

Wendy saw she could begin to accept her individuality and offer her opinions because she chose to, rather than to be controversial. And she could be proud to contribute the uniqueness of her thoughts and beliefs as a protagonist, rather than constantly waiting to hear what others thought, and then expressing the antithesis. If her opinion was the opposite of others, she could express that with her own authority, rather than antagonistically.

The affirmations she chose were "I am able to trust", "I have the right to my individuality".

CASE STUDY 2

Carol was a 27-year-old woman who chose royal blue/royal blue. She had studied for much of her life, and had a university degree in communication. She took this focus because all her younger life she had difficulties with communication, and believed that if she majored in this subject, it would teach her how to apply this skill.

However Carol is now in the workplace, and is very uncomfortable taking up her own authority and expressing her opinion. She works mainly with men, and said sometimes she is reminded of the times when she was small with her father, and he would not take her seriously.

At work Carol finds herself being very sharp in her communication, and believes she is sounding either too forceful, or goes the opposite and is too quiet. She is stressed and feels a lack of inner peace.

Carol had a childhood where her father was the dominant figure in the house. His authority was paramount and his word was law. Carol was the 3rd child and often this child becomes 'lost' in the family. This situation may be characterised by difficulties with communication, difficulties mixing with other children, and often being more comfortable alone with their inner-world. They can experience loneliness or being 'lost' in group situations.

This is why Carol had no experience as a child in communicating with family members. In addition, by having her father completely dominating and overpowering the domestic situation, she saw to perceive men as authorities and women as subservient. Her mother did as her father wanted. Carol did not feel safe in her father's presence and felt her peaceful existence was disturbed when he arrived home.

She suffered through the thoughtlessness of her father's words and she did not want to inflict the same dominating thoughtlessness onto others. However, in thinking too much about her words and not trusting herself to speak, she found that the appropriate moment had passed. This left her later thinking about all the things she should have said and did not.

Because her father's word was law she was in the habit of either expecting others to be the authority, or becoming the authority herself. She could not find the middle ground and a peaceful place. Carol was challenged around communication and needed to deal with this issue in order to have a satisfactory and fulfilling life both at work and personally.

Carol needed to become comfortable expressing her opinion and trust that the way she spoke was not 'too much', or thoughtless. Part of her process was to join a group of people with similar communication difficulties, where each was supported to express the story of their lives, and what they would like to have said in various situations. Each person kept a personal journal, where they expressed what they wanted. Within the group they were encouraged to say what they needed to express. The feedback given to participants was particularly useful because they could gain practice and confidence.

Carol could learn to trust that she would be safe as an authority figure, and use her power and words with integrity.

The affirmation which appealed to Carol was "I have deep inner peace".

CHAPTER 16
VIOLET

Violet contains hidden red and blue.

Violet suggests you are perfect as you are even if you are different to others. Violet offers the opportunity to heal the past, and supports you in dealing with the grief of hurts never healed, regrets unspoken, love unexpressed, and any unfinished issues in your life.

Violet people often have a quiet bearing and dignity. They are unassuming, and without airs, and find contentment in helping others. Violet children may be shy and not enjoy being in the limelight

There is a deep sense of equality within violet which says we are all the same, no one is more important than another, we are all human. True violet has self respect and thinks well of itself. In this way violet shows respect to others, and wants to uphold the dignity of all.

Violet says to remember that you are here for a reason, that you are seen and appreciated, and are perfect as you are with all your faults. Violet says you are not your behaviour, and don't lose sight of the fact that you are enough just the way you are.

Leaders, popes and generals often wear violet. True leaders realise they are servants of the people, and are there to serve the best interests of those they are leading, not to serve their own personal best interests. True leaders want liberation for their people, whom they recognise as brothers and sisters within humankind. Violet can be about caring for others and serving the community, and with this, violet is about humility.

Violet contains the possibilities for humility or grandiosity. The grandiosity of undeveloped violet says, 'I am the one you should respect, I am the leader, what I say goes, and I don't care about you.' Grandiosity is pretentious and will humiliate others by acting in a superior manner. Grandiosity shows no respect, and wants to keep others humbled. True violet is unpretentious, modest, humble and happy to be of service. They recognise the difference between being humble and being humbled. The difference between humility and humiliation. Between being of service and being a servant.

Violet can reveal an unavailable father or mother, and a subsequent sense of loss. Violet people may be very private people who perhaps have difficulty sharing their pain with others. With violet there is a suggestion of some unresolved feelings of grief. Because there is some discomfort when they have these feelings, violet people often disassociate, disappear, or do not want to be here. They can shut down and go inwards.

Grief is the reaction to a loss, and loss is part of the human experience. The loss of a job, home, lifestyle, relationship, youth, love, school, friendship, family, social life, freedom, income, support, mobility, health, a dream. This grief can be disenfranchised, that is to say no one really supports you because the loss is not recognised and validated. The experience of loss is an individual experience, which can only be measured by the one experiencing it. Each loss matters.

Those preferring violet can believe they are not understood, so tend to keep themselves private and hidden. As children they could have been ridiculed or shamed for being different, consequently violet individuals often believe they don't belong. They try to fit in, but think they don't. This can create a sense that they are invisible, or that no one really sees them. Violet can believe they are not enough, and would be noticed if they were 'more' in some way. Perhaps if they were more perfect. Violet people can strive very hard and put themselves under pressure.

Violet has a presence, and frequently you feel better just being around them. You feel healed in some way. Violet people may be vulnerable, sensitive or shy, and often think they are overlooked, that they are expected to care for everyone else, and no one sees them. Because of this violet can need to balance caring for itself as well as caring for others.

Hidden anger and frustration can be revealed in violet. Because violet people can feel shame around their anger, they often stifle it or disassociate when they feel it.

Violet individuals can have high ideals and want perfection. Consequently they could be very hard on themselves by trying to be super-human. Violet may need to learn that we are all human and all make mistakes. For violet people it can be difficult to make a mistake, they feel shame or not quite right if they do, and often try harder and harder to 'get it right', get it perfect. When they take off the pressure of getting it right, and therefore of being right, they can achieve great things because true violet has no limitations.

Violet individuals are sometimes difficult to be with, as they expect perfection not only from themselves, but also from others. It can be a struggle trying to live up to these high standards. Violet could learn this; 'if I don't expect myself to be perfect and accept I am okay as I am, then I can be with you and we can share our humanness, our humanity.' 'I am not better than you are, nor less than you are, we are all the same, we are all equal.'

As already generally discussed in Chapter 1, expecting yourself, a child, or another to be perfect is a set-up for failure, because nobody is perfect, we all make mistakes, as we are all human. We are all human beings with the possibility of learning and growing. Learning by definition means that we don't know, so to expect our children and ourselves to know what we don't makes life extremely difficult. To shame a child by expecting them get it right the first time and never make a mistake, sets up behaviour where they have to look like they know everything and can't show their fallibility, humanity and humility. We are all fallible as human beings.

If the script says that children and adults are not 'okay' when they make a mistake, they can be under enormous stress not to make a mistake, or not to be seen making a mistake or they would feel intense shame. A mistake can include showing a feeling if feelings were not allowed or accepted. Some learnt scripts say that feeling sensitive is equated with weakness. Some learnt scripts say showing fear means you lack courage. There are scripts that say we don't deserve to have joy in our lives, when in reality joy is our birthright. Our feelings are part of our aliveness, and if the child's script says 'don't have feelings', how can a child experience total aliveness? If we learn as children to cut ourselves off from our emotions and our aliveness, it leads to adults who feel they are only half living. The stress and the spiral of these beliefs and subsequent behaviour, can become intolerable.

Can you imagine the strain of trying to live your life the way someone else has told you you should be? Can you imagine the predicament of living your life trying to be someone else's idea of perfect in every moment, and rarely being able to be yourself, your actual self? That is like constantly being in a role. And all the time knowing there are parts of you that have not, and possibly will not, grow into fullness and be expressed. Maybe you live with this yourself. Think about it for a moment. Do you find you are too hard on yourself? Do you expect yourself to be perfect, the ideal wife, friend, mother, father, grandparent, child, teacher, employee? Trying to meet unreal expectations is extremely stressful. There has to be way, and the way is choices. We have the ability to make choices. Not by trying to change yourself, or your relationships, but to begin to see what it is you really are gifted at, and giving that. Violet offers the opportunity to re-evaluate our script, and learn to live again.

Sometimes we can cling to the past behaviour even if that is uncomfortable, because it is what we know and it is familiar. One of the reasons for this is that if we let go of what we know we have to enter the unknown. Violet shows that we can be at the point of changing and transforming our lives, or having grief for the past and letting it go. Throughout our lives we are continually transforming, with natural completions and evolutions. It is a part of life to learn and grow.

With violet we can see that the energy we put into the old script can go into our new choices. We can revise our script changing any narrow thinking or tunnel vision and old beliefs. This energy we have tied up in fear of making a mistake, of trying to be perfect, of being what others want and expect us to be, can then go into doing that which we were meant to do in the world. What is that? The answer is, you know, deep inside you. The memory of which we really are never goes away, our starlight does not disappear. Just because you cannot see it, does not mean it is not there.

No one else can tell you. You know. Our intuition was given as part of us, and we can learn to trust our deep inner knowing. These steps of transformation are all part of normal healthy growth through the stages of childhood and the stages of our life, where we gradually get a sense of ourselves and begin to trust there is a purpose for us.

Violet offers the opportunity of letting go of what is lost, and honouring what remains.

AFFIRMATIONS
I HAVE THE RIGHT TO MAKE MISTAKES
I AM PERFECT AS I AM
I AM GOOD ENOUGH

CASE STUDY 1

Sam, a teenager of 17 was rebelling at college, having difficulties with his studies, and was not sure what he wanted to do with his life. Sam said he was stressed and under pressure because whatever he did it was wrong, and he could never get it right. At first he did not want to speak. He was sad and not sure why he felt so bad and different. Sam chose violet/blue.

Sam expressed that he was having challenges with authorities at school and at home, and was very depressed about his life. He said he did not want to work in the manner his father, Patrick, works and spend so much of his life away from his family the way Patrick has done. His mother Jan was disappointed with Sam as he was the only son, and she expected Sam to be 'a good boy', the perfect son, and make the family proud of him.

Sam said he did not know who he was or what he wanted. He felt shame about being different, and shame about being 'bad', and yet he did not want to be 'good' and be unhappy all his life. Sam felt no real contact with his father, and was stressed trying to please his mother. So he rebelled.

Because Sam selected the combination of violet and blue, we spoke firstly about the blue in terms of his difficulties with the male role model portrayed by society. We discussed his difficulty in coming to terms with wanting to be a 'good' person, but seeing 'good' as a life which would deny his individuality, and put him on the same work path as his absent father Patrick.

Sam came to see that he does not need to be 'bad' to be noticed, or need to express himself in this way. He wants 'good' attention, but not to have the same expectations imposed on him, that were imposed on, or chosen by, his father's generation.

Talking through the violet issues, we spoke about the expectations he put on himself to be perfect and never make mistakes. Sam needed to talk about the way he dealt with this issue previously by trying to make mistakes all the time. He realised he was being a rebel, and through 'making mistakes' he wanted to see he was still okay even though he was not 'the perfect son'. The way he said it was, 'if I am this bad and make this many mistakes and you still care about me, you must really care about me'.

We spoke about the fact that nobody is perfect, we all make mistakes and this is a normal part of growth. I spoke about Michael Jordan the basketball player, and the way he used his mistakes as practice to hone his skills. This had quite an impact on Sam, and the pressure eased. He could see his 'mistakes' as part of achieving his desired goals. Sam realised he is okay when he makes mistakes, and he does not have to try to be the 'ideal' person. He need only be himself, and this is enough.

Sam saw that his value as a man does not lie with being successful in the eyes of society, but in contributing what he genuinely has to offer. He could see that his script said to be manly he must act in a certain way, which was contrary to his values and ideas on how he would like to live his life. We spoke about his Startree and his values, and what is important to him, and it gave Sam the understanding that he could live each day according to what he believes truly matters. This gave him a sense of personal power. With this foundation he had no need to rebel and Sam found he enjoyed his studies.

Sam realised it is okay to be different, and want to contribute in a different way. The affirmation he selected was "I have the right to be different".

CASE STUDY 2

Christine, a 26 year old married woman was concerned at being exhausted and angry. She chose violet/red. She did not consider herself an 'angry' person and felt shame at being this way.

Christine described herself as a dynamic individual, and yet for the past few months she had been suffering from action burnout, and then feeling frustration at having no energy. When we talked Christine revealed that she believed she was trying to be the perfect wife and yet underneath she was angry with her husband Jason, and embarrassed to talk about it to anyone.

Christine's marriage was not happy, and she believed her husband was treating her like a servant. She thought Jason did not see her most of the time, and that he did not understand her. Instead of looking at these issues, she would often go vague and 'foggy in the head', or make herself busier and busier, until she dropped down exhausted at night. This was her way of ignoring situations that were really worrying her.

Christine thought she was 'running on empty', and not sure of how to regain her drive and dynamic approach to life. When she realised how unhappy she was in her marriage, and how frustrated she was with this situation, her anger, once expressed, subsided. We discussed anger being a normal feeling, which if not acknowledged would come out in other ways.

Christine said she needed to make some decisions regarding her life and not rush headlong into 'anything and everything', like she did with her marriage. She said that she wanted to care for Jason, and she wanted him to care for her also. She wanted a more equal partnership. Christine realised her energy needed to be channeled into the life she wanted, and not wasted doing many things that had no meaning to her, but which kept her too busy to look at the reality of her situations. Christine expressed an understanding that hiding from life by being very busy, was actually depriving her of her real purpose in life, and the genuine contribution she had to offer.

We discussed some of the qualities of red, where they can often jump in quickly, and also give up quickly, and they need to see whether they are reacting or responding. Often the violet way of handling problems is by ignoring them and hoping they will disappear, or pretending they are not there. This often leads to an escalation of issues, rather than resolution.

Christine had previously handled problems in one of two ways. The red way was where she reacted by blaming the other person, then insisting they do something immediately or she would leave. Or the violet way, where she hoped the problem would go away. Either way she was stressed.

So rather than being hasty and leaving the marriage, we discussed techniques to resolve the conflicts without blaming. Christine decided to talk to her husband Jason and say what she needed. Jason was unaware of what had been in Christine's mind, as he believed she wanted to do all the things she did for him. With time he began to understand Christine's point of view and they could come to agreement around how to balance their lives together.

Christine chose to work with the affirmation "I am positive and determined".

CHAPTER 17
MAGENTA

Magenta contains violet, blue, and red.

Magenta needs to know they are cherished. They need to show love to themselves, and realise they are deeply loved in every moment, and allow the nourishment of this deep love to bring them to their own brilliance. Magenta needs to show as much compassion to themselves as they do to others.

Magenta children are deeply loving, empathetic and caring. Magenta is charming, graceful, delicate, and refined. They know how to beautify life.

You know when you are around a magenta person, because they will show you loving attention. A challenge for magenta can be the fact that others don't show the same level of attention to caring in small ways. This can cause magenta to feel frustrated and unloved. Magenta can have the sense that, 'I do all this for you, and you don't notice me'. Magenta people do not require great displays of affection; it is the small loving gesture that counts with them.

Magenta is deeply sensitive, and could have been shamed around their sensitivity. Magenta may need to know it is a gift to be sensitive. Magenta can believe 'my thinking is right, and my feelings are not'.

Magenta shows meticulous attention to detail, which can be a wonderful attribute, but it becomes difficult if they are trying to reach ever increasing levels of superiority. Magenta can be hard on themselves expecting to get every tiny detail absolutely right. They expect themselves to be ultra perfect, and struggle to meet impossible standards. This can be disruptive in their lives.

Compassion is a focus of magenta. When children are shown compassion if they make mistakes, when they understand they are lovable and okay no matter what their behaviour, then they receive something which is a priceless commodity. Magenta says support children to be themselves, so they will not have a life struggling to keep up with ever changing standards, or standards that were practical in a past time with different sets of circumstances. The concern about failing can be a driving force with magenta.

Encourage magenta individuals to have a rich and fulfilling life doing what they like and do best. Magenta says you are deeply loved and have the ability to achieve great things. Magenta reminds you that if deep love and caring is a mainstay, you will always know you have done all you could do. Magenta illustrates a need to realise we all have limitations as human beings.

Magenta is deeply caring and needs to show as much care to themselves as they so willingly show to others. Magenta people can be very precise, and are deeply sensitive to beauty in their surroundings, and these two qualities combine to reveal someone who is wonderful at anything which requires beauty in detail, for example, a designer. One of their gifts is creating a place of exquisite appeal by the love they put into the details.

Because of the refinement of their nature, loudness and brash display often embarrass magenta. The undeveloped magenta can be raw and crude, behaving with crassness, and stepping on the sensitivities of those around them.

Magenta shows a warm, giving and gentle individual who is highly protective. This protection taken to extreme can point to dominance in the guise of love, the smothering of others. Magenta can believe that when you give love you should get it back, and wonder why others don't show as much love to them as they show to others. Magenta can be seductive in an endeavour to get the love they so desperately need to fill an unloved place deep inside. Perhaps there is some hidden frustration and resentment around not receiving the love they give so freely.

The undeveloped magenta shows superiority, and gives the message that 'I am immaculate, unblemished, and spotless in every way, and you are second best, defective, and not good enough'. Magenta can have difficulty in admitting to faults.

Magenta can expect themselves to be flawless, impeccable right down to the last details. Magenta suggests that if you struggle to be the faultless friend, or mother, or wife, father, employee, student or child, then be more kind to yourself. Take it easy. Magenta supports you to know you deserve to be loved, as you are with all your faults. You are not inadequate or faulty; you are enough, whole and complete as you were created. You are gifted in your own way.

Within magenta it is possible to have a sense of being alone, yet embraced by something more. This is an exquisite, loving and caring sensation, and not always easily expressed. When magenta is in this place there is no need to talk as you can feel the love. Others want to be in the company of magenta to share the quality of this beautiful experience. It can be difficult for magenta to describe this wonderful deep place of love and beauty to another, consequently not many people understand magenta's depth.

Magenta suggests you find an inner place deep inside that you have just for yourself, a place of deep peace and love, and freedom from doubt. The other side of this is a sense of being utterly alone and unloved in the world. This is a deeply lonely experience. And this experience is extremely difficult to articulate.

A magenta individual who suffers from a sense of emptiness, needs to remember that you are here for a reason, and you are meant to be here, and your existence has meaning. You matter, and deserve to be loved exactly the way you are with all your faults. There is a place for you, and you are enough just the way you are.

Magenta often experiences a sense of abandonment. Children know when they are wanted and welcomed, and they can feel wrong in some way if the parents weren't ready to have them, or if they were born too early in the marriage, or too late in the marriage, or if parents had two children already, and you were the unwanted third. Sometimes it is said openly in the family that they wanted a boy, and even if it isn't spoken, the girl child knows it. They know there is something wrong, and believe it's about them.

Another form of abandonment to a magenta child is receiving love, but not the kind of love they need. The magenta child can experience abandonment when it is required to be the friend or companion of the parent to replace a missing parent, whether the parent is at work, or moved from the family situation in any way. Very often they were not loved for being who they are and they can have a hidden belief that you need to give love to get love. This is different from being able to receive love and let that in to the deepest part of themselves where they need it.

The magenta child, suffering from a sense of abandonment when one parent is absent, may believe that the absent parent is the hero, and life would be better if that parent was here. The magenta wife and mother perhaps feels frustrated, as her needs for love within the marriage are not being met because her husband is often at work, leaving her as the one to play both parent roles. In such a situation maybe she has difficulty giving out love all the time. Magenta instinctively knows what others deepest needs are, but are not always able to get their needs met. They need to care for themselves as well.

Magenta poses the question, 'what can we do for children, and for ourselves?'

We can learn something new and offer that to children. We can offer ourselves compassion for what we did not know before this moment, and choose another way of relating to ourselves, and to children. We can respect them for who they are

AFFIRMATIONS
I AM NOW DEEPLY LOVED AND CARED FOR
I AM LOVED AND WANTED
I NOW SHOW MYSELF COMPASSION

CASE STUDY 1

Karen, a 21-year-old woman was feeling totally unloved, repressed, and unsure what to do next. She chose magenta/magenta. All her life she had felt like she was not quite right in some way, and that she did not fit in with her family. She struggled to be faultless and do the right thing by everyone, and still felt shame. She said she felt empty inside.

Her parents had always wanted a girl and they had two boys, Mark and Noel, before Karen was born. The difficulty for Karen was that she knew she was not the type of daughter they wanted. She was pampered and treated like a doll, always on show and never able to be real. She felt smothered, tightly bound, and unable to have the full depth and breadth of her feelings. Karen felt frustration and resentment towards her parents because she could not be who she was; she had to pretend to be what they wanted. She said all her life was a sham.

Karen also felt guilty because of all the love her parents, Daniel and Melanie, gave to her, and not to Mark and Noel her brothers. In fact what happened to the boys in the family was that they were treated cruelly with many physical hardships and punishment. This punishment would take the form of being hit, and it was often carried out in front of Karen, which was shaming to her brothers, and also shaming to Karen because she felt very uncomfortable at being set apart and above her brothers.

The paradox was that instead of believing she was above and better than Mark and Noel, she believed she was less than they were, and unloved for who she was, and totally alone. There was an implied threat when her father, Daniel delighted in hitting Mark and Noel in front of her. Karen had the sense that if she ever stepped out of line, and was not the type of daughter her parents wanted, then the same physical punishment could befall her.

All her life Karen had believed that if she was not 'good', then she would be rejected and severely punished like Mark and Noel. So she went along with the pretence, and felt lost and unable to live her life.

She believed to be full of life was wrong, and yet knew that she was only having half a life with this pretence.

Karen experienced abandonment because Melanie and Daniel wanted her to be someone she was not, in order to fulfill the need they had for the daughter they imagined before she was born. All the love they heaped on Karen was only if she pretended to be this imaginary daughter. In fact she did not feel loved at all, and still believes her parents would not love her if she behaved like her real self. She played the role they wanted. She felt shame at who she really was, as though this was not enough.

This is abandonment because the needs of the child are secondary to the needs of the parents. Many adults behave in a certain way with their parents, and believe they cannot be who they really are. They feel shame if they are who they really are. So when they see their parents, they go into the role that would please their parents, and become someone other than their true self. This pattern of behaviour is often set up in childhood.

Karen needed to begin to express her true feelings. She had difficulty with anger because she only knew the anger of her father towards Noel and Mark, and Karen said she did not want to be like him. We discussed the difference between her feeling of anger, and the behaviour of Daniel.

Karen came to see that anger is one of the feelings we are given as human beings, and is the energy for change and movement. Anger gives us the ability to say 'no', and restores our dignity. In fact Karen was not able to express the anger she felt when she was totally denied the possibility of being the child she was. When she named the anger and saw that it was okay, Karen said it was as though a weight was lifted from her.

My experience of Karen in the beginning of the session was of someone who was weeping, frustrated and experiencing a lot of shame at saying who she really was and what she wanted for her life. When Karen understood that she was not expected to behave in a certain prescribed way, that she could be herself and express whatever it was she needed to say, she came to life. It was as if she woke up.

We discussed that every child deserves to be loved the way they are, and Karen could understand that although she received a lot of love, it was not the kind of love she needed. It was a relief for her to know she did not have to pretend anymore, and yet it would take practice for her to behave as she really is and reveal that to others. I encouraged her to be compassionate towards herself when she made mistakes, because it would ease the belief that she had to be faultless and superhuman.

Karen had lived with shame all her life, shame that she was not okay as she was, and that she would not be loved if people knew what she was like deep inside. To overcome this Karen needed to practice being herself and revealing her true colours. She needed to be encouraged to lead a more meaningful and fulfilling life doing what she liked best.

After doing her Startree Karen had more of a sense of what she wanted to bring to her life, and by taking one value at a time and using it each day, she became more practiced at owning who she was. Living her own values, and making a difference to the lives of others this way, was the antidote to the pretense she had previously lived.

Karen needed to learn she was lovable as she is, so she used the mirror technique of looking into the mirror each morning and evening, and saying to herself "I am lovable as I am". It was strange for her at first, and then gradually became easier. Within about five weeks Karen noticed the difference, and she believed the way she walked and carried herself was different. She felt less shame, and lighter.

Karen came to understand that she was perfect just as she had been created, that she was a star with her own special light. When she gained this understanding, she began to learn to show the kindness and gentleness to herself, that she showed to others.

Karen chose to work with the affirmation "I am lovable as I am", "I can now have my life".

CASE STUDY 2

Rebecca, is a nineteen-year-old girl deeply upset about the fact that her boyfriend has left her. She chose magenta/turquoise. She does not feel she will be able to live with the indescribable loneliness she is experiencing. She has always had difficulty describing to people how she was feeling, and the harder she tries to explain now, it seems the less they understand. She was feeling desperate. Rebecca expressed a loneliness no one else seemed to understand. She believed she was unlovable and utterly alone, sometimes found in magenta.

Rebecca was a deeply sensitive person who said she had tried so hard to please her boyfriend, because she had no one else in her life. Whatever her boyfriend Keith suggested they do, she went along. She went to football games, car racing and boxing and watched endless sport on television when she had no interest in sport. They spent time with his friends where she often felt uncomfortable because she was unused to mixing socially. Keith was frequently busy with his interests, so did not have much time to spend with her. She was so grateful for his attention when she received it, that she did not question the relationship, as she saw Keith as her hero who had come to rescue her from a life of loneliness.

Rebecca's father was a distant figure because he was always busy at work, and her mother was angry most of the time. She had felt really alone in the world from the beginning because her mother did not want her, and indeed her mother did not want to be married to her father. As a little girl Rebecca knew this, because her mother was always speaking in a detrimental way about her father. In fact her mother did not have a good word to say about her father.

Rebecca said that as a child she loved her mother, and wanted her to be happy and did everything she could to please her. But her mother did not, and still does not want Rebecca's love. The truth is, her mother does not want Rebecca at all, and blames her for the fact that she had to stay with her husband. Rebecca has been told all her life that if it is was not for her, her mother would have had a wonderful life, and it is Rebecca's fault that she has missed out on so much and is so miserable.

As a small child she believed her father to be a distant hero, and she fantasized he would come home and rescue her from her mother. Rebecca thought that if he knew what was happening to her, he would do something about it, and save her. Whereas in fact the truth is, there were arguments when her father came home, so life was unhappy then and she would hide or read, or imagine that this was not really happening. She dreaded the company of her mother the next day after these arguments, because her mother would vent her anger on Rebecca, who could not be perfect enough. No matter how hard she tried to do everything just the way she knew her mother wanted, she would not be able to escape her mother's rage.

To cope with the unloving and lonely life she was experiencing as a child, Rebecca escaped into a world of fantasy, where she would be safe with the heroes and heroines in her books and magazine, and on television. Real life in her world was unbearable, with no escape in sight, so she created another world, where she could have everything she needed, in just the way she needed it. When the arguments happened, she would enter this world of her imagination, where she was loved and safe. It was her only respite.

When she met her boyfriend, it seemed that at last in her life she had found someone who wanted her. What she did, in fact, was place her fantasy onto this relationship, and make Keith the hero who had finally come to save her. She did not see Keith for who he really was during the relationship, which was a repeat of the pattern with her parents.

Rebecca repeated this script, because this was all she knew and expected from life. When Keith left, the huge loneliness she felt before, returned. She felt very lost. This was in a sense the repeat of her life when her father came home briefly and she expected something wonderful to happen. When it didn't, she experienced the reality of the loneliness and sense of abandonment in her situation, which she alleviated with her fantasy world, a combination of turquoise and magenta possibilities.

We discussed the abandonment issues of magenta which she was expressing, the indescribable loneliness, and sense of being unloved and unwanted. What Rebecca had never known was the fact that there is a place for her in the world and that she was born for a reason. We spoke about her life having meaning, and the uniqueness of the contribution she could make by being herself. It was necessary for her to understand that she was not alone, and that she mattered, and that she deserved to be loved not because she had pleased someone else, but just because she was born. She did not have to please anyone to be loved; she is lovable the way she is. These were totally new concepts for Rebecca who was amazed to have this information.

Turquoise individuals can escape into a fantasy world, the world of their imagination. This rich inner world may be expressed as an artistic quality, and is part of the individual contribution of turquoise. Rebecca needed to be encouraged to express herself, and not live her life only in her mind. She began to keep a journal, and discovered a new sense of freedom and relief at expressing her feelings, thoughts, and experiences from throughout her day. She also unearthed her gift for creative writing.

Rebecca saw she needed to begin to start new relationships, to expand her life, and ease the sense of loneliness. So she joined a group of people who were interested in creative writing, and found there were others with similar interests. This opened a door to an understanding of a greater world to which she belonged.

She used her creativity to think of phrases that she would like to hear, to show how loved she was. She came up with phrases like "Rebecca, I love and care for you", "Rebecca, I am happy you are in my life", "Rebecca, you are welcome in my world", "Rebecca, you are an extremely good creative writer". She wrote these on small pieces of paper and placed them where she would see them through the day. For example, she carried one in her wallet, and even though the piece of paper was folded, just the sight of it reminded her that she had cared enough for herself to place it there.

It was the beginning of a totally new internal experience for her and her true beauty began to emerge. The affirmation she chose to work with was "I am beautiful and lovable, and I matter."

CHAPTER 18
DEEP MAGENTA

Deep Magenta contains all colours.

Deep magenta holds the potential for everything within its grasp. Undeveloped talent is often lying dormant and unmaterialised within this colour.

Deep magenta is able to see a world of different possibilities. They can be inspirational to those around them

These individuals see a lot that is hidden within others, often being aware of people's deepest issues. Highly insightful, deep magenta recognises the unrevealed capabilities within another individual. They seem to be able to uncover that which is special in others. However they cannot always see themselves. They may remain an enigma to themselves and others, and indeed they can enjoy displaying a degree of mystery.

They are deeply understanding, and could wonder why people do not understand them the way they understand others. They may be perceived as being complex or involved.

Deep magenta is very loving and caring, with the likelihood of wanting to rescue those in distress.

Perhaps they need to know how valuable they are, and apply the same degree of caring to themselves. Very often they are unsung heroes, who have the tendency to minister to the needs of others, and can experience exhaustion.

Deep magenta points to an underlying intensity, and they may be forceful, compelling individuals, who are somewhat hard to fathom or extremely private. They can be content working behind the scenes as a driving force encouraging others to fulfill their latent skills.

Deep magenta is able to materialise the unseen and bring about change. They have a multiplicity of talents which are often suppressed or undisclosed.

Others perceive deep magenta as a strong force, capable of great feats of endeavour. They are resolute and staunch, and a good person to have on your side. Because of their tendency to become concerned and involved, they can become overstrained and depleted.

Deep magenta says 'you are not alone, you are where you are meant to be, right here, right now at this point in your life.'

A richness of quality is displayed by these resourceful individuals. Or in the undeveloped deep magenta, much can remain uncultivated and unrealised.

Deep magenta indicates how things manifest in the small details of your life.

These individuals are astute at discerning the unexplored potential of those around them, and as such deep magenta is a great motivator, helping bring out concealed talents. Deep magenta points out the need to bring forward your own undeclared talents too.

Deep magenta says, 'it looks very deep, but you have the resources and capacity to plumb the depths.'

The possibility for renewal and change at the very deepest level is held within deep magenta. A total transformation.

AFFIRMATIONS
IT IS NOW SAFE TO REVEAL MYSELF
I HAVE RICHNESS AND DEPTH WITHIN ME
I APPRECIATE MY QUALITIES

CASE STUDY

Emma is a 35-year-old woman with two small children, Alex and Chris. She had recently divorced and was struggling to believe her life had any purpose. She wanted to believe in, and trust men again after the unhappy experience with her husband Mathew, but was unsure. She chose blue/deep magenta.

Emma wanted to trust that her future could be different, and to find some peace in her life. Instead she was driven and busy and unable to relax or stay still for any length of time. She believed that if she did, she would be overwhelmed by a deep depression, and expressed feeling alone and lost in something and could not find her way out.

When she talked about her life, this lack of trust and inability to be peaceful was a recurring pattern. Emma recalled that as a child she felt unwanted and lonely even though there were four children. Because she was the last child she was unplanned and unwanted, and had not received any attention from her father Brian.

The family was aware that their father had relationships with other women, and as a little girl Emma came to believe that men could not be trusted to be there when you needed them. Her father Brian was a distant and remote figure, and Emma chose a husband who was the same type, repeating the pattern.

As a small child Emma would be busy at home trying to be 'good' by taking care of everyone to get attention from her mother Marion, who was attending to the other children, with no time to communicate with or care for Emma. She had a sense that if she spoke no one was there to understand what she said, so she did not say anything. This set up loneliness (a blue issue) and a pattern of rescuing others (a deep magenta issue). The way Emma coped as a child was to do many things for everyone to keep her occupied, a deep magenta trait.

We worked with the many possibilities and undeveloped potential hidden and unrecognised in deep magenta, so that Emma would have a sense of herself and hope for her future. She was uncertain about her worth because of the childhood experience, so this was an important issue to cover. When we spoke about her life having meaning, and that there was a reason she was born, and that no other person could contribute in quite the way she could, it started Emma thinking about her values, and how she could take steps with these. She felt empowered.

We worked with the blue issues of a need for peace, and to have faith in the process of her life, and that all men were not like her father. She could have entirely different relationships than those she had experienced.

Emma came to see her life from a different viewpoint and slowed down. She was keen to use affirmations and to say them to herself when she began to become hyper busy, as a way of bringing calm and peace within herself. The affirmations Emma chose were "I have faith and trust in the process of my life", and "All is well in my world".

CHAPTER 19
CLEAR

Clear reflects all colours.

Clear has no limits; it has the possibility for everything.

Clear is the light that reflects every colour of the rainbow. When you look at a piece of crystal, you often see rainbows reflected from it. So the clear person has the possibility for all colours within. Clear has a purity, innocence and simplicity.

It is an enriching experience to be around a clear person because they have deep clarity. To others, clear can make the unclear obvious. Usually clear people are very clear about what they want, or they can get foggy and unclear.

The experience for a clear individual can look like this. Because they have a sense of each of the colours within them, they can be very comfortable with all people, and become a mirror to others. When you are with a clear person you will have a sense they see things from your perspective, and are aware of how it is for you. And they are. This is because they have a sense of your colours and your viewpoint inside them.

Often clear individuals can feel lost, and seem to always be looking for something, something that reflects them, somewhere they can get a sense of their identity.

Frequently they are really attracted to someone, or to a job, or a hobby, and then find it very limiting, very one dimensional, as they are unable to express all they can be. And they can become bored. Clear may be seen as a jack of all trades and master of none, because of their experience at many things

The challenge for a clear person is that they can see others clearly, and others cannot see them and this can cause suffering. It is not easy for other colours to understand the clear experience, because you see them through the eyes, of blue, or green, or red, etc., whereas clear can see you through the eyes of the rainbow. Clear often experience relief when someone sees their situation from a clear viewpoint. At last someone can mirror back to them their life experience, instead of being always the mirror for others.

Clear can feel the emotional pulls in the group, so they need to be certain as to which of these emotions are theirs.

Clear suggests you ask yourself, 'what have I learned from the difficulties in my life that I can now shine as a light to others'. Clear says, 'appreciate yourself by recognising there is a certain nobility in suffering, that your suffering has meaning, and that there is no further need for suffering.' It is not a sign of weakness, it has taken courage. Suffering ceases to be suffering when we become clear about it, and see what we have gained. Enlightenment often comes with it.

Clear offers the possibility to see clearly. It is an opportunity of clearing patterns of beliefs we have had in our lives since childhood. Maybe unconscious beliefs mirrored by the mother or mother figure, and taken on at a very early age, even pre-verbal. Clear shines the light on the subject.

Clear can be the need and the opportunity for the clearing of emotions. If children are not allowed to cry, it is as if their tears become frozen. So clear can represent frozen feelings from childhood that are waiting to be cleared now. These issues come up for resolution when we are safe in our lives. The paradox is that when our lives are going well, there can be lots of unresolved issues that come up because we are now secure and safe enough to resolve and release them. It may be described as the ice melting and washing the pain away, washing that place clean. Often we avoid pain or tears considering them weak. Sometimes people won't allow themselves to cry, because they feel that if they started crying, they would not be able to stop. It is a natural process to cry, and can be clearing and cleansing. Tears have a beginning, a middle, and an end, and are a normal and natural part of the human experience. The gift of pain is healing and growth and connection with our vulnerability and humanity.

If the clear in your colour combination is with blue, it can indicate feelings were initiated by blue issues, which may include those of communication often held in the throat. This combination could also indicate you have a need to be nurtured. If the clear is with green, it can be pain held in the heart; or in pink, pain about the need for unconditional love; in gold the pain could be because you were not valued. To gain more insight for yourself, look at the issues that are in the Chapter on the colour which is combined with clear in your selection.

The other form clear can take is being added to another colour creating a paler version of that colour. For example, the addition of clear to blue, will create pale blue, and to green it will create pale green, to yellow it will create pale yellow, and so on. There are many pale colours in the colour combinations, so check yours.

The addition of clear to the colour will then intensify the issues of the colour it is with. So pale blue would intensify blue issues, pale green intensify green issues, and pale yellow intensify yellow issues. Clear added to red makes pink, so pink has the possibility of intense red issues.

Many of the hidden beliefs that we hold unconsciously are based on powerlessness, hopelessness, and worthlessness. Have courage. The rewards of seeking the light of your own star are great. Commit yourself to your healing so you can accept crisis and pain as an opportunity for change and growth. Each time you have the courage to embrace yourself and heal, you will discover more harmony within, until you are free to react in an appropriate, spontaneous and compassionate way based on your truth, rather than the influence of the past.

Clear suggest living in accordance with your genuine sense of self, your unique authenticity, and sharing that with the world.

AFFIRMATIONS
ALL IS WELL IN MY WORLD
MY WAY IS NOW CLEAR
I AM CLEARING THE PAST

CASE STUDY 1

Anthony is a 17-year-old teenage boy working with turquoise/clear. Since early childhood Anthony had a sense of not being understood, of being alone in a vast empty place where no matter how hard he tried he could not fit in. Parts of him seemed to be able to relate to others, yet mostly he felt desolate and unable to feel comfortable with people.

He was not sure where he fitted in the world, and was unclear about who he was and where he wanted to go. He expressed a sense of desolation where suicide was the only escape. He believed death could offer no worse emptiness than life. He was not sure which career suited him; he was interested in various options, but not really enthused about one in particular.

Anthony was the only child of very busy parents who were never there for him. He said he wanted to share his thoughts with his parents Ed and Alice, but they were always in a hurry and did not care about him. Anthony expressed himself by painting and drawing, but his parents thought this was a waste of time for a boy who should be thinking of a career leading him to be as successful as they were.

Since he was young, Anthony believed that he was not quite masculine enough or the businessman type like his father Ed. It was not his interest to follow in his father's footsteps, and Anthony could see no way out.

We talked about his right to be different, and to express his individuality in the way that suited him. Anthony needed to understand that his creativity was a gift, and that this could be expanded to embrace a career which would be fulfilling for him, and add to the lives of others. By gaining a sense of the gifts of clear, Anthony saw how much he had to contribute, and, importantly, he came to understand how many people he did get along with, rather than how many he did not get along with.

Anthony came to view his life in a much more positive way as soon as he understood that 'different' equals good, and not 'different' equals desolation and rejection. Instead of viewing his life as empty, he saw the other side of clear, which is limitless.

Anthony was enthusiastic about the technique of making a cassette recording of all the individual qualities he possessed. He listed his positive qualities and gifts he had to contribute, and using his creative flair combined various musical sounds behind his voice speaking on this affirmation tape. To create the tape Anthony was using his creative mental qualities. Anthony also used his artistic gifts by painting how he really wanted to see himself in four years from now. This was an exercise in creative visualisation, where Anthony could envisage the life he wished to have with him at the centre of it. Anthony liked the idea of updating this painting from time to time

He chose to work with the affirmations "I can see clearly now", "My way is clear", and "I have the right to be an individual". Anthony used his artistic qualities to create affirmation statements in the colours important to him, and placed these around his room.

CASE STUDY 2

Bonnie was a 23-year-old woman who was having difficulties with her marriage. She chose clear/green. She could not settle down and yearned for something, which she could not describe and which her new husband Steve could not understand. Bonnie wondered whether she had made a mistake in getting married, and yet she had believed that marriage was just what she needed to give her a sense of belonging. She expressed an intensity about her deep need for 'something'.

We discovered that Bonnie had certain beliefs about marriage, where she thought her husband Steve should be all things to her, and provide her with a sense balance. He was supposed to meet her every need, while she could have freedom to do what she wanted, and still be married.

Bonnie said in her childhood there was no space for her, she was the eldest child and took care of others, and yet believed she was 'less than' them, because their needs came first. Bonnie was waiting for a prince charming to give her everything she did not have as a child, and fill the emptiness she felt inside her heart. When this did not happen, and Steve could not fulfill her needs before she became aware of them herself, Bonnie wondered if she had made the right choice, and should she move on and leave Steve.

We discussed the clear issues of emptiness, and in this case, it was with the green issues of Bonnie's heart. She had never felt that she mattered at all, and the emptiness was like a big hole inside her heart waiting to be filled. We talked about how this' filling' could happen for Bonnie, and how she could attend to this herself, rather than unrealistically expecting someone else to do it for her.

Bonnie released a great deal of unexpressed and frozen feelings that had been stored since she was quite small, and expressed relief that she could share some of this childhood desolation, and not have to carry it for the rest of her life. Bonnie said that as a child she was afraid of being overwhelmed and lost in this emptiness, and by expressing some of the feelings now, she became less afraid of having feelings in the future. She spent most of the session crying about this emptiness, and realised it was not her marriage that was empty at all.

Bonnie came to understand that Steve was not to blame. The more she became clear about what she was unconsciously expecting, the less Bonnie felt like running away from the marriage. By becoming aware that she was running away from her unhappy childhood, and by expressing how it had been then, there was no need for Bonnie to keep running in her life generally.
We talked about the gifts Bonnie had through green, and

the gifts with clear, and the less she compared herself, and came to realise the possibilities within, the more freedom she had inside. The desolation was not in her life now, because she did love her husband, and wanted to be with him. Bonnie stopped comparing her life to others.

Bonnie decided to use the affirmations "My life is rich and full", "My heart is open and free" and "I am generous and kind".

CHAPTER 20
CONCLUSION

So how can we make the world a better place for children ensuring that they are filled with hope and a sense of their worth?

We can do this by ensuring they know they are cherished and loved just the way they are, and by encouraging their difference and supporting them to express that. We can have them follow a star value on their Startree so they become aware of their individuality, and realise they can make a difference when they are choosing how they want to respond to life's situations. Use the insights you have gained from within the colours to foster and nurture your child's gifts, and encourage them to contribute those gifts every day.

Remember these keywords: -

Support	Inspire
Listen	Teach
Love	Encourage
Care	Trust
Forgive	Cherish
Nourish	Thank
Nurture	Accept

Believe in yourself, your worth, your uniqueness, your preciousness, your contribution.

Remember that mistakes are a necessary part of learning and growing.

Do not judge yourself. Do not judge children.
Do not compare yourself. Do not compare children.

Open your heart.

Trust. Trust yourself, and trust that your life has meaning. Make your Startree your goal posts and your stars your goals.

Recall the power of words, and notice the type of thoughts you are habitually thinking, and the words you habitually say. Create other words. Use the words in your chosen colours. You can create the world you want.

Use your affirmations each day. Perhaps you could carry them on pieces of paper in your wallet, and say them as often as you need. Each time you see the piece of paper you are reminded of who you are and your true value and worth. Say your affirmations first thing in the morning and last thing at night.

Put your affirmations where you can see them, maybe even inside your cupboard, so that each time you open that door you will remember this is what you chose to say to support yourself in your life. Say your affirmations whenever you are in doubt, to remind yourself of your grandness and worth and value. Look through the affirmations in all the colours each day, and see which one you think you need, and say that. Look in the mirror each morning, look into your eyes, and know there are no other eyes like yours on the planet, no other face like yours, no-one quite like you. You are a star, say your affirmation while looking in your eyes.

Care for yourself. Care for children.
Encourage yourself. Encourage the children.

Remember that we are created with feelings for a reason, and no feeling is wrong, they all have a gift. Which gift is your feeling endeavouring to give you? Trust yourself and care for yourself on a day when you have resistance to change, allow yourself to be where you are in your life. Permit yourself to be fallible, and know you are not alone. Permit children to be fallible, and let them know they are not alone.

Be grateful for what you have. Get a diary and write five things in it each day for which you are grateful, and this will change your day and your life, because your focus will be on what you have, rather than what you don't have. What is special for you? Whatever it is, write it down in your gratitude journal at the end of the day. It could be a sunny day, a rainy day, the smile of a child, the kindness of a friend, anything at all that has value to you. Have your child do the same. Demonstrating to a child the value of gratitude encourages the understanding that no matter what is happening in our lives, we all have something to be grateful for. And we can miss out on the experience of gratitude, which is one of connection. Connection to yourself, connection to others, and connection to the world around us.

Shame is something that is learned by children. We all need healthy shame to tell us when we have stepped outside our values, and when we do this there is a need to apologise, and learn from the experience. Without healthy shame we can treat others inhumanely. Healthy shame teaches us that we are all human, we all make mistakes, and there is a humanity and humility in this. Unhealthy shame occurs when we are ridiculed, humiliated, made fun of, or put down as children, and we learn to believe we are faulty or wrong, or 'less than' in some way. We become shame bound, and will experience shame whenever a similar situation occurs. This is called toxic or unhealthy shame, and it limits and restricts the lives of many adults and children. Shame is passed from generation to generation.

A child can be shamed at any time because of its body, perhaps it is said he or she is too short, too tall, too fat, too thin. Or perhaps they look different by wearing glasses or different clothes or have different hair. When the child is shamed it comes to believe there is something wrong with its body or the way it looks. This child grows into an adult who believes they will never look good enough, and he or she has to look a certain way to be acceptable. They must look any other way than the way they do. This is being shame bound around body issues.

This is an extremely common situation with both males and females, and they become prey to advertisers telling them they will lead happier lives if they wear these particular clothes, or shoes, or have this hairstyle: 'You will be more attractive if you wear clothes with this label'. 'We will show you how to be more appealing if you change the colour of your eyes, the shape of your face, lose weight, gain muscles, or eat this food.' 'You should wear these sunglasses, wear this cap, buy these jogging shoes, buy this car, smoke this cigarette, then you will look good and be successful.'

Shame is found in the colour red, and red is hidden in pink, orange, coral, gold, royal blue, violet, magenta, deep magenta and clear. So there could be hidden shame issues in pink around needing to be heard or loved, in orange about the need for connection with other people, in coral around wanting love to be returned. In gold perhaps there is hidden shame around self worth or issues of intelligence; in royal blue about thinking differently; in violet about not being perfect enough and being different; and in magenta around not being wanted the way you are. There are other possibilities suggested within the chapters on each colour, so use this to gain insight into your own situation.

If the child was shamed around its thinking, and was told 'you are stupid', 'what would you know you are only a child', they can become shame bound around their thinking, and will not want to share what they think to anyone, certainly not in group situations. This is often found in gold or royal blue.

If the child was shamed around any of its feelings, and learned that some feelings were good and some bad, they will experience shame whenever they have this feeling. For instance some maps of the world, some learnt scripts can tell a child 'you must not feel fear, you are weak if you do', so the child will believe they are wrong if they experience this perfectly normal and healthy feeling. Every feeling brings a gift, and fear teaches us, bringing the gifts of discernment and wisdom. Fear alerts us to danger and shows us when we need to take care of ourselves.

If we were not meant to have feelings as human beings, we would not have been created with them. Each feeling is energy, and if the energy of this feeling is blocked, it is locked in the physical body and stored in muscle tissue or organs, or the energy comes out in other unpredictable ways.

When we become bound by the unrealistic shame we learned as a child, it is like an unseen energy which restricts us from our true self and potential, and what we have to give. If the child was shamed when it felt angry, it can believe that anger is wrong. Remember that anger is a feeling, not a behaviour; it is what you chose to do with the anger that is important. Remember that feelings have a beginning, a middle and an end and the expression of the feeling to yourself is often enough, without the need to do anything more. The anger might be telling you that your dignity has been offended by a situation and you need to acknowledge this to yourself. Or the anger may be telling you it is time to use the energy for change. Often someone is angry if they have been offended, hurt, violated, or believe something wrong has been done to them, or to something, or someone else.

Healthy anger says, 'no', 'you cannot do that to me, or anyone else'. Anger restores your dignity, and that of others.

Anger is found in the colour red, and remember that red is hidden in deep magenta, magenta, violet, royal blue, gold, orange, coral, pink and clear. Generally a child feels angry because it is not heard, not noticed, not loved, not accepted, not wanted, or not given time and attention. Children have inalienable rights, and they know when they have been offended. Maybe the child is angry because it was not loved unconditionally, and this is a possibility in pink; maybe the child feels angry because it is not wanted or cared for, and this can be in magenta.

The child has the right to its feelings, and often because the feeling cannot be expressed it gets locked in. This is why so many adults find freedom and relief in saying, for example, 'I was not wanted as a child', and expressing the feeling now. Maybe the feeling is pain or sadness. Often when we are safe and secure in our lives, the old feelings come up to be released because we are now in a safe position to experience them.

If a child was not wanted, it can become shame bound around its existence. It can feel shame around being born at all, and that it destroyed something worthwhile. Examples of this may be if the child is a boy when the parents wanted a girl, or a girl when they wanted a boy, or 'we have two children and there is not enough time, space or money for a third child'. Maybe the child is not wanted because it was born too soon in the marriage, or too soon after the child before, or too late in the marriage, or too late after the child before. The child will know it is not wanted because of the parent's attitude to it. In some families the child is told it is not wanted. Either way the child then carries a burden of shame throughout its life.

These possibilities can be revealed in green, the complimentary colour to red, where the child will always compare itself in situations, and come up 'less than'. They can feel guilty for taking up the time of their parents. There is a possibility in gold where the child will have a lack of self-esteem and self value. This issue is possible in orange or coral where the child can feel a level of trauma living with its parents who do not connect with it. It is traumatising and very frightening for a child to exist in a place where he or she cannot connect with the warmth of other humans. Royal blue has the possibility because this child can feel utterly alone. The colour clear can reveal pain and emptiness in its life. In violet the child can feel different and not understood. In pink it could feel unloved and unheard. In magenta the child is not shown the kindness and caring it needs, and the utter desolation of the child is possible in deep magenta.

Some children were shamed when they expressed needs, so they are shame bound around needs. Every human being whether adult or child, has the need for love and acceptance, the need to be heard, to be affirmed, and to receive time and attention.

Shame is a big issue.

The intention and benefit of this book is building better relationships with children. It is about teaching by example, by showing children how to love, cherish and respect themselves, and giving them hope. Listening to children can give them a sense that they matter. Children are not born believing they don't belong.

A child needs acceptance, reassurance, patience, nurturing, protection, containment, touch, safety, unconditional love, acknowledgment, discipline, attention and respect. A child needs consistency so trust can develop. It needs to be reminded of its positive qualities more than the negative. It needs to be affirmed and upheld. This book is about upholding the worth of each person, and the importance of validating his or her value as an individual. It is about saying it is important that you are here.

'How can I use the information from this book in the world in my life?' First, by remembering you are here for a reason and your life has meaning. It does not matter who you are, or what you have or have not done in your life up until now, your life has meaning, and you were created for a purpose just the way you are.

Secondly, look at your Startree and your values, and see how you would like these expressed in the world, and live life with these values as part of who you are. Do not try to make radical or drastic changes, but listen to yourself and get a sense of what is inside you. Begin to explore other possibilities that feel right for you. The possibilities of what you really have to contribute in your life. And grow into doing that which you were meant to do in this world, and do it. Do it. It is part of the experience of life, the possibilities that we were all born with. The possibility of realising our true colours and giving those to the world every day.

No one else can tell you, you know. Our intuition was given as part of us, and we can learn to trust our deep inner knowing, and break the old chains that bind us to something we have outgrown. Take it step by step. These steps are all part of normal healthy growth through the stages of life, stages of childhood, where we gradually get a sense of ourselves and begin to have faith.

Remember you are a Starchild, you come from the stars, and you will return to the stars having shone your light and contributed in your own special way on earth.

> Every child is a starchild.

Bibliography

Bradshaw, J. (1988) *The Family*, Florida U.S.A.: Health Communications Inc.

Bradshaw, J. (1988) *Healing the Shame that Binds You,* Florida U.S.A.: Health Communications Inc.

Covey, S. (1996) *The 7 Habits of Highly Effective People,* Melbourne, Australia: The Business Library.

Frankl, V. (1984) *Man's Search for Meaning*, New York: Washington Square Press.

Goleman, D. (1996) *Emotional Intelligence*, London: Bloomsbury Publishing.

Kubler-Ross, E. (1974) *Questions and Answers on Death and Dying*, New York: Macmillan Publishing Co. Inc.

Mackay, H. (1998) *The Good Listener*, Sydney: Pan Macmillan Publishers Australia.

Maslow, A. (1993) *The Farther Reaches of Human Nature*, U.S.A.: Penguin Arkana.

Mellody, P. (1989) *Facing Codependence*, New York: Harper Collins.

Scott Peck, M. (1985) *The Road Less Travelled*, London: Arrow Books.

Zukav, G. (1990) *The Seat of the Soul*, New York: Simon and Schuster Inc.

For details of Rickie's workshops and sessions, or to order this book please call 0402 257654 (Within Australia) or +61402 257654 (Outside Australia)

ORDER FORM

Name ……………………………………...…

Address ……………………………………...…

………………………………………………….

Tel. Home……………... Work……….….……..

Fax……………….. Email…………………………..

No.of Books………..Payment includes post $………

For payment of $A24.95 each book plus postage:-

Card No:
Name on card   Expiry date   /

Cheque money order made payable to:-
  R. HILDER, PO. Box 941 Kensington, 2033 AUSTRALIA

**Fax + 61 (0)2 9399 9820   mobile phone 040 225 7654
            email   kwanyin33@hotmail.com**

Postage charges inside Australia   1 Book $5.50